The Sum of Us

A True Story of Love, Land and the Long Road Home

Elise Berenger

Copyright © 2025

The moral right to be identified as the creators of the work has been asserted by them in accordance with the Copyright, Designs and Patents Act 1988. All rights reserved.

No part of this book may be reproduced, stored in a retrieval system or transmitted in any form or by any means, electronic, mechanical, photocopying, recording or otherwise, without the prior permission of the authors.

Book Cover by Ven Visual

www.venvisual.com.au

Designed by Red Feather Publishing

www.redfeather.com.au

ISBN: Paperback 978-1-7644316-0-6

ISBN: Hardback 978-1-7644316-1-3

Contents

Where it all Began	1
Dedication	2
Foreword	4
Prologue	9
1. 15 to Love – Not Just Tennis	11
2. Courting on Court	20
3. Withdrawn	29
4. No Papers	35
5. Life-Changing Letter	42
6. Sisters	51
7. Unaccompanied	59
8. Johnny Nonsense	68
9. 15 and Fearless	76
10. Mountains of Love	88

11.	Corrections	107
12.	Eles' Gate Crash	117
13.	On Our Own	127
14.	Snapped	139
15.	Trespassing	147
16.	Hostage	153
17.	Pack It Up	158
18.	Farewell	166
19.	Escape Artist	175
20.	Four Missing Decades	187
21.	Filling in the Blanks	195
22.	Mum or Bomma	203
23.	End of an Erra – not a spelling error	210
Epilogue		217

Where it all Began

Dedication

To my wonderful family.

First and foremost, to my husband Johnny, my best friend, my soul mate. Thank you for embracing life with me, with all my craziness, wild ideas and harebrained schemes. Thank you, too, for the countless times you've quietly had to pick up the pieces when I've dropped the ball, and for all the late nights and crazy hours you've endured while I poured myself into not only my sculptures but these pages too. You have stood by me, encouraged me and cheered me on through everything I've ever attempted. Together we've weathered storms, laughed till we cried, and carved out a life full of love and adventure.

Without you at my side, this journey would never have been the same.

DEDICATION

And to my beautiful children; Renée, Daniel, Paul, André, Monique, Philip, Felicity and Antonio. You complete me. Thank you for your endless love and support, for being the joy in my every day. Sometimes I wonder at the way God has blessed us with such extraordinary, wonderful children. My hope is that this book will not only tell our story but also carry forward the legacy of where we've come from, our history, our roots, our heritage. May these words be a gift to you, to your children, and to the generations yet to come.

J + E = 8

Foreword

By Colonel Pat Armstrong (Retired), Rhodesian Light Infantry

One of the strangest days of my time as Officer Commanding Support Commando, the Rhodesian Light Infantry, came sometime in 1976. We were on one of our ten-day R&Rs when my old friend, Padre Bill Blakeway, walked into my office.

'Sir,' he began, 'I've got a welfare problem I need to discuss with you.'

I sighed and said, 'Bill, please don't make your welfare problems mine. Speak to my 2IC, Piet Farndell, or to the CSM, Phil Payne.'

But Bill wasn't letting it go. 'No,' he said firmly. 'I need to speak to you personally on this one.'

I replied, 'As I've just said, please don't make your problems mine.'

Bill smiled that disarming smile of his and pressed on. 'I've been approached by one of your troopies, his name is Johnny Berenger, you know him. He's keen to fight, but because he's only seventeen, he's stuck doing canteen duties when you go out on operations.'

I did know him. A good troopie, an olive-skinned, Portuguese fellow, though his name didn't seem to sound it.

'Bill,' I said, 'you know the law as well as I do. If he's under eighteen, he needs to have written consent from his parents.'

'He has no parents,' replied Bill.

'Then he'll need consent from his guardians,' I said.

'He has no guardians either,' said Bill.

'Then he'll have to stay in base until he turns eighteen. Simple.'

Bill looked at me for a long moment and said, 'I'm afraid I'm about to make this problem yours.'

'What do you mean?' I asked, already dreading the answer.

'Berenger and I have decided that you will be his guardian.'

I stared at him. 'That's ridiculous. I'm single, I'm twenty-seven and I can already see the paperwork nightmare. I'd have to justify this to the authorities and somehow convince them I'm suitable for this important role. It'll never pass muster.'

Without missing a beat, Bill reached into his folder, placed a stack of completed and witnessed forms on my desk, and said, 'Please Sir, just sign where indicated.'

I laughed 'Bill, this is absurd!'

I was bowled over. He'd already done it all. He had managed to convince the authorities and had completed the paperwork. Somehow Padre Bill had made it official. I tried one last time to wriggle out of it, but he fixed me with that determined look and said quietly, 'Sign, Sir.'

So, I did. After all, I respected him too much to say no. Suddenly, I was officially the legal guardian of Trooper Johnny Berenger.

When we called Johnny into my office and explained what had happened, he wasn't the slightest bit surprised. He and Bill had cooked the whole thing up between them. Typical. He stood there, looking utterly pleased with himself; a determined young man who knew exactly what he wanted.

Before dismissing him, I said, half seriously, 'I've no idea what my duties as your guardian are supposed to be, but my main interest is that you stay out of harm's way, and most importantly, do NOT get yourself killed.'

'Yes, sir,' he said smartly.

'Good hunting,' I told him, and that was that.

We didn't have much to do with each other after that conversation, though we served in many of the same operations. He was a brave, reliable and capable young soldier.

Interestingly, our paths parted on the same day. My final Fire Force contact with Support Commando was in the Mtoko operational area on 15 May 1977, a long, intense, and successful engagement, though we lost two men that day: Trooper Earl Macdonald, a close friend of Johnny's, who had just turned eighteen, on his first and last contact, and also Trooper George Clarke, who was shot and killed right beside Johnny.

Johnny left the Commando the very next day, having completed his three-year service contract. I was posted to Army HQ. We never saw each other again.

Years later, in South Africa, my wife Mary and I attended a braai [1] at the home of a mutual friend. Among the guests were Johne Fletcher, who had been an officer under me as Colonel in the Selous Scouts, and his wife Phee. The Fletchers and Berengers had been neighbours in a farming district in Zimbabwe, and Johnny had shared the same extraordinary story with them. The name stopped me in my tracks. I realised it was the same young man whose life I'd once been responsible for. They knew that.

They told me he was now living in Australia. I wasn't sure if he'd want to reconnect after all those years, so, regrettably, I didn't contact him then.

---

1. A South African term for 'barbeque'

Many years later, Elise contacted me, and so, Johnny's story, found its way back to me. Most recently, I was delighted to have a long video call with Johnny. It was emotional, to say the least. After all these years, it felt like closing a circle that had been open since 1976. Elise, Johnny and I have now reconnected, and I couldn't be happier for it.

I've immensely enjoyed reading this memoir. Thank you, Elise, for finding me and sharing this incredible story. It was an honour to serve with brave, fearless men like Johnny. He was a determined, loyal soldier, and now, through these pages, a man whose extraordinary life of courage, survival and heart will not be forgotten.

Prologue

Right from the first time I met Johnny, he would always lament and say, 'I wish I could write.' More on that later.

To all those – who have listened to snippets of our story over the years, and who have said, 'You really should write a book,' this is the result of that gentle (and persistent) persuasion. Over time, I've carried these memories in my head, scribbled them onto bits of paper, and stored half-finished files on the computer. Finally, now, the time feels right to gather them all together in one place.

I wanted our children and the future generations to know more about where they come from and to understand their dad's remarkable journey; his life growing up in two completely different worlds, without the family structure and support almost everyone takes for granted.

A great deal more life has been lived since I began writing the odd pieces down, and the story has now unfolded across decades and continents. It has become a long, tangled but colourful story.

At first, I thought I'd try to write his story through my eyes and ears. Then I considered asking Johnny to narrate it himself. But as I've heard him retell events over and over again, with that same sparkle in his eye and slight embellishment with every version, I decided the best thing would be to write down the story as I've seen it, heard it and lived it.

Although Johnny's story isn't a fairytale, at times it has certainly felt stranger than fiction. His story is of survival against all odds, enduring the traumas, the chaos of war and the heartbreaks with a stubborn resilience, miraculously defying death more times than seems fair.

Somewhere along the way, when our lives collided and became one, the story has been as unpredictable as it has been wonderful. Love can change everything ... and sometimes we 'speak things into existence.'

1

15 to Love – Not Just Tennis

Before we reach the pivotal embassy visit, which was the point at which this whole story comes together, there are many things that must be told, but they need to be told out of order. So, if this story seems to leap backwards and forwards, please bear with me. Sometimes, in order to understand the heart of things, you need to follow the tangled threads. And tangled they certainly were ... and still are! Kind of like a big bowl of spaghetti, where there are definite beginnings and ends, which are not always visible. The many lines criss-cross over each other, touching in many places.

I grew up in a lovely, leafy suburb called Groombridge, in Harare, which is the capital city of Zimbabwe, located in the country's north–east. Back then, most of those Harare suburbs had big, rambling gardens with colourful flower beds dotted around wide expanses of lawn, perfect for wandering about barefoot. Often a big jacaranda tree would stand proudly, making a purple carpet beneath when the blossoms fell. If you were lucky enough to have one near your driveway, it was always delightfully satisfying to hear the popping sound of the flowers as the car tyres ran over them.

Looking back to when I was just seventeen, fresh out of school and standing at that crossroads of life, I honestly had no clue as to which path I should wander down. I could quite happily picture myself as a farmer's wife, because I had fallen in love with every single farm I'd ever visited. The open skies, the huge gardens, the smell of the soil after rain, the rhythm of farm life – it all called out to me. The only problem was that I didn't have a husband, and I most certainly didn't have a farm. Alas! (But hold that thought ... it will be significant later.)

So, not having a farm nor the faintest clue as to what to do with my life, I looked around and grabbed the first opportunity that sounded remotely interesting, which was a course at Harare Polytech. I had always loved art and was quite taken with the idea of their Graphic Arts section. Did I know what on earth I might ever use it for? Absolutely not, but a couple of my friends were already attending and suggested I might enjoy it as much as they did. That was enough, I made the decision and headed off to have a look around the Polytech. The place buzzed with creativity and energy, and it certainly seemed like a lot of fun. I gathered together some bits and pieces of artwork and submitted my little portfolio. I had said to myself, that if I wasn't accepted, then I'd know this wasn't for me. I had an interview with the director and was promptly accepted. Before I knew it, I was off on this new adventure.

The course turned out to be brilliant. I loved it and met a whole circle of new friends from a variety of backgrounds. But if I'm honest, there wasn't that big pull that said, *Yes, this is your life's direction.* When the first year was done, I was done too. I couldn't see myself continuing on for any longer, so I pulled out.

Meanwhile, there had been another option dangling in the air: a tennis scholarship in Post Falls, Idaho, United States. I tried to imagine my life in a country that I'd only heard about and seen in the movies or on TV. It sounded wonderful, and hugely exciting, and I was very tempted to accept, but deep down I knew myself well enough. The idea of waking up every single day and *having* to play tennis... well, let's just say, I didn't really think I would cope with that. Also, my parents were not in a financial position to enable it, so the offer was politely declined.

I've always loved being active and keeping busy. With every sport on offer at my school, the Dominican Convent in Harare, you could be sure I was there, kit bag slung over my shoulder, ready to go. Hockey, basketball, swimming, diving; I played them all. I was even honoured with the privilege of representing my country in both Tennis and Hockey in the U18 schoolgirls' team.

A highlight was receiving a certificate to state that I had a 'world ranking' of 87 for tennis in my age group. It felt a little surreal at the time, but as I look back on it, I realise the honour to be chosen to play for Zimbabwe was not just about the sport, it was about carrying a flag for all the hours of practice, the encouragement from coaches and family, and the sheer joy of playing the games I loved.

Those opportunities gave me confidence and a sense of belonging that went far beyond the tennis court or the hockey field. Many of my connections and friendships were formed through playing sport and they have lasted a lifetime, especially among my tennis crew. I'm still in touch with most of them today, all these decades later.

Tennis was my first love, and as it happens, it's also where I found my true love. Do you know that old saying? *In tennis, love means nothing.* Well, that didn't hold true in my case.

Towards the end of my A-level year, just before I began the Graphic Art course, I found myself at a tennis festival in Mvurwi. (pronounced mvoo-Rwee) Originally known as Umvukwes, Mvurwi was a vibrant and prosperous farming area about a hundred kilometres north of Harare. It was a close-knit community where everyone seemed to know everyone, and life revolved around the land, the crops, the weather and what was going on at the club.

I had participated in many of these types of festivals from about age fifteen. They were held every couple of months, each one hosted by a different tennis club for a whole weekend of tennis matches, laughter and catching up with familiar faces.

For the country festivals, local farming families would usually host visiting players, and that particular weekend I ended up staying with Mick and Liz and their lovely family. Little did I know then that they and their farm on Forrester Estates would be part of the same close farming community that would become our world after Johnny and I were married.

The Mvurwi club was a special place. The clay courts were some of the best around, always perfectly rolled and maintained, kept in top condition for the many junior tournaments, league matches and lively annual festivals.

The playground was always alive and buzzing with children's laughter, (my own kids would one day fill these spaces just like then), and the cheerful chatter of maids keeping an eye on them while their parents played a match, added to the friendly atmosphere. Tall fir trees lined the playground fence, casting cool, dappled shade, while further down past the tennis courts, the rugby field and pavilion sprawled out and, beyond that, the polo grounds. It was truly the heart of the Mvurwi farming community.

The festivals were always a wonderful gathering of players from all over the Mashonaland district. Some families would make a whole weekend of it, camping around the courts or along the edges of the nearby golf fairways and greens.

The tennis itself was brilliant; competitive but full of good humour. The real charm lay in the social side. Long chats between matches, gentle teasing between rivals, plenty of laughter from the bar, and the inevitable lively Saturday evening party. And let's not forget the incredible spread of food that accompanied the entire weekend. Plenty of home-baked cakes and puddings galore, endless cups of tea and, of course, the wonderful catering by Lycharny, the club's cook, and his loyal team. Lycharny was a great character. This short, cheerful African fellow with a towering white chef's hat and crisp apron was always bustling about with a grin and a joke. No matter how many mouths there were to feed, he somehow managed to conjure up delicious, hearty and flavourful meals.

That September weekend, I'd won my division, which should have been cause for great celebration. The Mvurwi club had an enormous rounded wooden bar. Doors opened up onto the veranda, looking out across the pristine green cricket pitch on one side and then the 18th green of the stunning golf course on the left side. It was a friendly and inviting design. The snag was that I was still under eighteen and legally not allowed into that great bar where everyone gathered afterwards.

To be fair, I doubt whether anyone would've thrown me out if I'd wandered in, but my shyness kept me lingering on the edges instead, happily watching all the goings-on. I hovered near the disco area, which was in the little side lounge area, where the DJ, a man with a very large moustache, was playing songs from what I considered to be a *very questionable* music collection. He was blasting out one Dolly Parton hit after another, with Kenny Rogers thrown in for variety. I was convinced those two were the only artists in his entire LP stack: Dolly and Kenny, Dolly in Concert, Kenny in Concert and the rest!

What I hadn't registered at the time was that this moustachioed fellow had also played in the tournament. He and his best friend Richard Cross, along with another mate called Mini MacDonald, had been right in the thick of the weekend's fun. The banter in the clubhouse, the joking around after matches, and of course, a fair number of beers downed. They were larger than life, while I stayed watching quietly in the background.

Little did I know that this very DJ, Johnny, would one day change the course of my life. And as fate would have it, those two friends were in fact the ones who'd first dragged him into playing tennis. Funny, isn't it, how things begin?

Almost without my realising it, during that year, my life's path began to stretch visibly out in front of me.

Let me rewind a little, because while tennis and moustached DJs were bubbling away in the background, I was still a seventeen-year-old girl with absolutely no clue as to what I wanted to do with my life. While I tried to sort myself out, I took up some volunteer work at our church bookshop and library. It gave me something useful to do with my time, keeping me connected, and gave me a quiet space to think and to breathe.

After the volunteer work, I eventually landed my first job, at an architect's firm, working as a draughtsman (or draughtsperson, as we'd politely call it now). A family friend, Marlene Swanton (God rest her soul) had suggested it might suit me, and I thought, W*hy not?*

So, armed with nothing more than enthusiasm and a love for drawing, I handwrote letters to every architect's office in Harare. And when I say 'handwrote,' I mean it. No typewriters, no computers, just me, an ink pen, and my very best handwriting on fancy letter-writing paper. I explained to them that I'd always loved drawing and painting, and even mentioned how, back in Standard 2,

I'd won a school competition in Maths to design a house. My dream house, no less! Sunken rooms, big bay windows, oversized rooms – it had the works. I'd even managed to make the plans more or less to scale, complete with sections and elevations, all on one enormous sheet of paper.

A couple of firms responded to me, and I was invited to go and visit them. I still shudder when I think about my interview with those two architects, Mr Martin and Mr Wales-Smith, by whom I was eventually employed.

There I was, proudly laying out this very amateur blueprint, as if Michelangelo himself might nod with approval. It was, in truth, more like a three-year-old showing Mummy a stick drawing and calling it a portrait. But somehow, they were impressed. Not so much with the house plan itself, but with my handwritten letter. They said it was the neatest handwriting they'd ever seen.

I can still picture myself sitting at our dining table with my fountain pen and bottle of blue ink. I had the Dominican Convent to thank for that. Years of being drilled, that penmanship had to be immaculate. Perfectly straight letters, tidy, and utterly legible. There was no Tippex in sight. I'd simply start again with a fresh sheet of my special writing paper, every time I made a mistake, striving for that perfect, immaculate script. Oh, if only the Convent nuns could see my writing now - no thanks to smartphones and keyboards. I can't imagine gaining employment today on the strength of my handwriting, as it is barely legible, even to me.

However, back then, it opened the door to my very first job. And just as my professional life was finding its footing, that moustachioed DJ kept crossing paths with mine, like a thread weaving into the patchwork of my story.

I've always found it fascinating how lives twist and tangle, how people appear in your life in the most unexpected ways. You think you're meeting someone for the first time, and suddenly you realise they know your cousin's old school friend, or they once played cricket with your brother. In Zimbabwe, they say there are five degrees of separation. Honestly? I'd argue it's more like two.

When I left that Mvurwi festival behind, little did I know that a future tennis festival weekend would bring another layer of surprises, laughter and connections that would shape the next chapter of my life.

2

Courting on Court

Fast forward to another tennis festival, this time hosted right on my doorstep at Old Georgians Club, conveniently situated just across the road from my family home. By then I was no stranger to the OG's courts. I'd been playing tennis there almost every Saturday since I was about eleven, whether it was a few sets of social, a league match or one of the weekend festivals.

Old Georgians was very much the club of choice for the old boys from St George's College. This was the school all my brothers had attended. It was always a hive of activity. The rugby section was particularly strong, producing a winning team year after year, and some of those players even went on to represent the country. Cricket thrived there too, with its fair share of stars. Hockey was buzzing as well, and I had played in a team there for a few seasons.

Then there were the squash courts and, of course, the swimming pool. My brothers and I loved that pool. We didn't have a pool at home, so it was our great treat to spend hours there on weekends or school holidays, whenever we could.

But, for me, the tennis courts were always the heart of the place. That's where I felt completely at home. Week after week, year after year, I played there, slowly getting to know everyone and becoming part of the OG's tennis family. Between the Saturday matches, the league games and the big festivals, that was where so many of my happiest memories were made.

And so, at this particular festival, when the Mvurwi club turned up with their team as they always did, who should reappear but none other than DJ Johnny.

By then I was eighteen and out of school. Finally, I was old enough to join in on the bar fun without anyone raising an eyebrow. As always at these festivals, Saturday evening was a lively affair; plenty of laughter, delicious food, dancing and the kind of easy fun that followed a full day of tennis.

Since Old Georgians was just across the road from home, I'd become used to strolling back and forth without a thought. Back then, it was still safe enough that no one batted an eyelid at a girl walking home alone, sometimes after dark.

As Saturday evening progressed and the meal ended, Johnny and I somehow got chatting. I was quite taken by this not-so-tall, dark, handsome man. He was making jokes and seemed to want to keep dancing with me. I distinctly remember his rock 'n roll moves across the floor, with him leading ... or rather, 'throwing' me, as I fumbled to match his steps.

Suddenly, it was past midnight, and despite my protests that I could safely walk by myself, I was driven home that night ... in a Mercedes-Benz, nonetheless! Johnny, ever the gentleman, insisted he drop me home and, oh my gosh, he even opened the door for me to get into the car. My dad, waiting up for me as always, was not impressed. Not just at the hour of my arrival home, but at the fact that I'd invited this mysterious, older-looking and darkish-skinned man to come in for tea. Yes – tea! But anyone who knows Johnny, knows he downs a gallon of it a day. Besides, there certainly wasn't much else in the house that I could have offered him, apart from some of Mum's sherry, possibly.

That night, we chatted for hours, getting to know each other. I also heard the heartbreaking news about Johnny's best friend, Richard Cross, the same Richard I knew from those fun-filled tennis festivals. He'd recently been killed in an horrific car accident. It hit hard as he and Johnny were housemates and had been together just prior to the dreadful tragedy.

Richard had been a very vibrant part of the Horseshoe farming community (a farming district adjacent to the Mvurwi area) and of the Mvurwi tennis crowd. It was hard to imagine a tournament or gathering without him. He and Johnny had been as thick as thieves, more like brothers really, and his loss had clearly left a deep ache in Johnny's heart. You could feel it. The whole community did. We didn't know it then, but Horseshoe would become central to our lives.

The next day at tennis, I saw Johnny chatting with someone who I didn't recognise and hadn't seen playing tennis. Just why he was there, I didn't know. Johnny then introduced me to this person ... his good buddy Patrick Scott-Martin.

The introduction was somewhat novel, and he casually said with a cheeky grin, 'This is the green chick I was telling you about.' I almost died of embarrassment. Had there been a rock to crawl under, I would have done so. Thankfully, my shy nature and good Catholic upbringing had kept me firmly on the greener side of the spectrum ... if you know what I mean. Most of that day, I noticed that when he was not on the court for his matches, he was a spectator at mine.

After the first exchange of phone numbers, there followed a whirlwind relationship and then, not even a year later, I found myself engaged to that very same DJ man. So strange how life pans out. At the time, of course, I had no idea. And, by the way, Patrick, would later stand beside Johnny as a groomsman at our wedding.

By then, I was a few months into my job at Martin Wales-Smith Architects, and Johnny and my friendship had already blossomed into something deeper. He was working as a manager on Govete Ranch and was a well-liked and respected part of the Mvurwi farming community. He was finding more and more reasons to be in Harare, so I got to see him fairly regularly. And when he wasn't in town, there'd be long phone calls, placed through the Mvurwi exchange on the party line. It's weird to remember those big black phones hanging from a board on the wall, complete with bells. I still remember the farm ring '2 shorts and 1 long'. Sometimes I would run to the phone on hearing our ring, only to discover it was actually Zilla, the African Grey parrot who had mastered it.

I spent most weekends out on the farm, and that's where I really got to see firsthand what a respected and successful farmer Johnny was. Acres and acres of crops spread out over the farm, lands planted with mostly tobacco and maize. I was always struck with amazement when I thought about the work that went into growing the crops. Every maize pip carefully planted by hand and every single tobacco seedling tucked into the soil, one at a time.

We'd make our way around the lands either on his motorbike or bumping along in the old short-wheelbase Land Rover. That vehicle was a boneshaker of note! With zero suspension to speak of, every rock, rut and corrugation in the road sent vibrations straight through your spine. By the end of a drive, you felt as though your bones had been completely rearranged.

Some days we made our way down to the farm boundary, ending at the most magical spot, where there was a bottomless pool. It sat at the base of a little waterfall on the Musengezi River, which wound its way along the bottom of the Mvurwi Dyke. It was the kind of place that felt like a secret paradise, perfect for picnics, swimming in the pools or just wandering about and exploring.

Often at weekends, neighbours would go down to the waterfalls too, bringing their friends and families. It was great fun to jump off the rocks and down into the cool water below, shouts and laughter echoing off the rocks.

Looking back, I can understand my parents' shock when our relationship had become serious, and there was mention of marriage just six months in! There was no real proposal; just talk and an unspoken understanding that we belonged together and should get married. Johnny still maintains that I asked him ... perhaps it was telepathy?

Now, when I think of our three daughters, I honestly can't imagine being happy about any of them wanting to get married to someone within just six months of meeting, especially at the tender age of eighteen. And let's not forget, Johnny looked, and was, much older than me at the time; he was twenty-seven. Things were different back then, and truthfully, when you know, you just *know*. I'd prayed about it earnestly and had recently been on an Ignatian Retreat to help me know what God was calling me to do. In the Catholic faith, it's quite common to go on a retreat at pivotal moments in life, when you're seeking direction, about to start a new job or to discern a vocation.

The centre was near Lake McIlwaine and became the perfect place to live in five full days of silence, without chatter and distractions. The days were filled with spiritual conferences, structured meditations, counsel from the priest and, of course, prayer and the sacraments.

Deep down, I felt at peace, that this was the right path, and he was the 'one'. Funny to think that there was even a time I'd considered a religious vocation ... yes, to become a nun! Clearly, God had other plans and a different kind of lifelong commitment in mind.

Things progressed quickly, and Johnny would drive into town, always bringing fresh fruit and vegetables from the farm. He'd fetch me from work and take me out to lunch when he had tobacco sales or errands to run in Harare.

When I went to the farm for the weekend, I would either sleep the nights at Hans and Shirley Maartens' home, in their cottage on Forrester Estates F section, or we would have my brother and his girlfriend tag along as chaperones. All our friends would make fun of this fact, but I wasn't going to have it any other way. This very farm, Forrester Estates F Section, where I slept over in the cottage, is another place that would play a big part in our lives, though we didn't know it then.

It was tennis festival time again in Mvurwi, only one year on from the first 'DJ Johnny' encounter … and we'd recently become engaged. My parents had insisted I turn nineteen first. They were struggling with our relationship. My poor parents … their only daughter.

My brother, Father Anthony, reminded me quite recently that I had asked him to persuade my parents to allow me to marry Johnny. His persuasion worked, and they eventually resigned themselves to the fact that their little girl was going to be marrying this 'older man.'

We had a quiet but beautiful engagement celebration at the Jameson Hotel. My parents, my brother, and his girlfriend at the time, all joined us. Our family friend Marlene, as she always did, was playing the piano in the lobby, and Gordon Adams (God rest his soul) was the general manager of the hotel. It was one of the *places to be* in Harare, and many night-outs and celebrations were held there. I couldn't believe that from one Mvurwi tennis festival to another, just a single year on, I was sporting a beautiful engagement ring. I could not have imagined a lovelier fairy-tale.

3

Withdrawn

'Where does he come from?' my mother asked. 'He looks so dark. Who are his family?'

Mum was at her wit's end. And that, right there, is the reason I decided that I should one day write a book.

Now, it's necessary to go back in time again, to untangle the reason behind the sudden withdrawal of consent, to discover what had caused all these doubts, and the darkness which threatened our story before it had even begun.

And so began the unravelling of the spaghetti.

I had just returned from work at the architect's firm to find my parents looking extremely concerned and anxiously waiting to announce something.

Then it came.

'We withdraw our consent, and you may not marry him.'

Hearing those words from Mum hit me like a tonne of bricks. It was absolutely devastating because only a few weeks earlier, Johnny had sat down with Dad and asked his permission to marry me, his only daughter.

As I was the second youngest of eight children and the only girl, they were understandably protective. And rightly so, I suppose. (Side note: I used to call myself 'Snow White' growing up with seven brothers, how could I not? I had even given each of them a dwarf name, though I won't share who was Grumpy or Dopey! Let's just say, the shoes fit.)

'Why? What's going on?' What could possibly have happened to make them change their minds? I simply did not understand it.

Both my parents worked at the bank, and Mum's position was in the Security and Investigations department. This meant she had access to a great deal of information on the known criminals and listed fraudsters around the country and the general 'baddies' about town.

As the mother of her precious *only* daughter, who, at nineteen, was ready to marry a man, nearly nine years her senior, Mum felt she needed to use her resources to do a background check on Johnny. Understandably, she needed to be sure this man, who had captured my heart, had no criminal history or other dark secrets lurking in the shadows.

I do remember Mum confiding to me in the past that people aren't always who they say they are. She knew that from bitter experience. In her younger years, she had been engaged to a man who turned out to be nothing but a charming and deceptive womaniser, stringing along several women behind her back. She could not let history repeat itself. She feared that the same might happen to her darling only daughter, all starry-eyed and talking of marriage.

She was ready to do everything in her power to stop it, should she dig up anything suspicious.

She began to do a comprehensive search in the records for Johnny, her future son-in-law, and that search led to a whirlwind of chaos.

She was horrified to find a 'shopping list' of entries against his name. I suppose, in her head, her worst nightmare was about to take place. Some criminal was going to ruin her daughter's life.

This shocking revelation came out of the blue and made no sense to me at all.

'He's not who he says he is. He's been married before. He's stolen things. We think he's a con artist.'

I was completely dumbfounded. My chest tightened, and my head started thumping. 'No! It's not true! It's just not true,' I pleaded desperately.

Dad didn't say much. He liked Johnny, I could tell, but I was his only daughter, and he too didn't want to see me hurt. Mum was adamant and without hesitation she declared that Johnny and I were not to see each other anymore.

I was gutted; my heart had been ripped out.

Breaking the news to Johnny was unbearable. He was devastated and completely bewildered. He couldn't understand it either and was terribly upset. He kept asking what was wrong and why my parents had turned against him? All I could say was that Mum had heard some really unsettling and concerning stories about him at the bank. Repeating it to him aloud sounded unreal.

I was breaking ... and so was he.

His farmworkers noticed the sadness in him, and that he was not himself. When I next saw him, his eyes were red and swollen, and his cheeks were lined with raw furrows from the rivers of tears. He couldn't make sense of any of this. He looked utterly broken, and I knew I wasn't far behind.

I begged my parents to believe me. I pleaded with them to trust what I knew ... that there was some mistake, and that Johnny was not the man these rumours painted him to be. Even though I hadn't known him long, I was certain of the goodness I had seen. Surely, if he were hiding something so dark, I would have caught a glimpse of it by now? A hint, a slip-up or some shadow lurking? And yet I had picked up on nothing at all. They say *love is blind*, but I felt absolutely certain he was a good man.

Eventually, my parents decided they should visit the farm and confront Johnny face to face, to hear his side of the story. I hoped this would help clear everything up. Naturally, I went along to the farm with my parents. Mum was absolutely determined to get to the bottom of what she had read about Johnny in the records. I sat in the garden confused and crying profusely, while my parents, mainly my mum, interrogated Johnny. It was just awful.

I was extremely anxious and half terrified that she might uncover some hidden monster, and at the same time almost certain that she wouldn't.

I kept wondering whether there was another side to this man that he was somehow hiding or that there was something I had missed. None of his friends had ever said anything negative about him. Surely Hans and Shirley, who had treated him like their own when he was managing F Section, surely, they would have known? Either they were covering up a terrible secret or it was all just a dreadful mistake.

He said, 'Ask anyone – ask my friends, ask the people who've known me for years. If what you've heard is true, they'll tell you.'

I believed him and, as always, I prayed for discernment and calm. For the truth to reveal itself.

After all the questioning and the discussions and earnest appeals, Mum finally, although reluctantly, relented. Dad, thankfully, was never quite as doubtful as Mum. He managed to persuade Mum to give Johnny a chance to prove himself.

Following on from that visit, the slow, fragile healing gradually began. It took time, but the thaw did come, and eventually by the time Renée, our first child, was born, Mum was completely convinced of Johnny's goodness.

But at this point, before our marriage, the questions, the whispers and the doubts were still there under the surface.

They were only the beginning.

4

No Papers

Back in those early days when Johnny and I were getting to know each other, discovering our childhood stories, over endless cups of tea and long walks around the farm, I learned that he had come from Madeira Island. I could tell there was a bit of a shadow there, as though there were some chapters he wasn't quite ready to read out loud. I didn't want to push. I mostly listened, carefully and with curiosity, and didn't ask too many prying questions. It was clear he'd had a bumpy ride growing up, and some of it still seemed raw. He usually changed the subject or made a joke.

He told me how he'd come to Salisbury (now Harare) at just twelve years old, to help his dad and brother with their little shops. I can't begin to imagine being that young and being forced to work. Somewhere along the way, something bad had happened, but he didn't want to go into detail. From what I gathered, his dad wasn't exactly up for any parenting awards. Apparently, he often drank heavily, and he wasn't very kind.

Eventually, Johnny said, he'd lost contact with his family altogether, and this resulted in his growing up in an orphanage. He went to Prince Edward School and left early, before completing any exams, and then he joined the army as a boy soldier. He was only fifteen and a half when he made the big decision to enlist.

By eighteen, he was out of the army and found himself working on a farm in Macheke, which was to be the start of his farming career. From there, he bounced around the farming districts, starting in Headlands, moving to Mvurwi and then to Darwendale, taking up various management jobs on different farms. He still kept a foot in the army, doing intermittent call-ups during these farming years, and he was also a member of the police reserve – in a unit called P.A.T.U. (Police Anti-Terrorist Unit.)

Later, he ended up back in Mvurwi, where he did a stint as a sales representative for Farmec (a farm machinery company). He then landed a management job on Govete Ranch, which is where I came into the picture. A couple of years before we met, his friends Mark and Mungo convinced him to join them on a trip to the UK and Australia. Many of the young men in Zimbabwe took a gap year before starting university or college. He was keen to join them on this trip, but there was one small hitch – he had no documents. No birth certificate, no passport, nothing. He did, however, have a driver's licence, which he'd obtained in the army – his only identifying document.

Now, this is where the story takes a wonderfully Zimbabwean twist. He popped down to the local passport and ID office in the nearby town of Concession. As he was able to speak fluently in Shona, he conversed with the official behind the counter there, probably cracked a joke or two and, voilà, just like that, he walked out with a passport one week later. No birth certificate required. The clerk simply filled in the details Johnny had provided to him:

Name: John Louis Berenger. Place of birth: Liverpool. (Liverpool? We're not even sure why. Maybe it was his favourite soccer team at the time. Who knows!) One thing I can say for certain is that this passport would come back to bite us, and honestly, it deserves a whole chapter of its own.

Anyway, off Johnny went, gallivanting around the world with his mates and living it up in true bachelor style, with all the pub crawls and late-night partying that came with it. There was even some shift work thrown in for good measure.

Mark and Mungo eventually continued on across to the eastern states of Australia, but Johnny decided to stay put in Perth. He'd been given a job at the Perth Yacht Club, and they seemed to like him so much, they had offered him full-time work. He was tempted to take up the offer, as the money was excellent. Who wouldn't be? But in the end, it wasn't the bright city lights of Perth or the sandy beaches that had pulled at his heartstrings, it was Obos, his Bullmastiff dog, waiting at home in Zimbabwe for him.

Whilst on his travels, Johnny had left Obos with Hans and Shirley to care for him.

Obos wasn't just any dog. He was a proper gentle giant, all muscle and heart, with a head the size of a lion and shoulders like a prize-fighter. His bark could make the windows rattle, but in truth, he was an enormous softie. Most of the local farmers knew Obos, as did all the farm workers, but as soon as someone who hadn't met Obos saw him, they were rightfully frightened, as was I, at first sight of him.

Obos was a remarkable dog - also with a story to be told. One day, just like that, he disappeared. We had searched and called and driven around the whole farm, looking everywhere for him. We had feared the worst as the days passed. We had pretty much given up all hope of finding him. But quite amazingly, eight long days later, he came stumbling back into the yard. He was badly cut and bruised, looking as though he'd been dragged through a thorny hedge. He was skin and bone and barely standing. But there he was, alive. How he had managed to find his way home is unfathomable. We were absolutely over the moon that he'd survived and returned to us.

As it turned out, he'd been caught in a wire snare somewhere on our farm, or possibly in the neighbouring communal farming area. He still had the remains of barbed wire snagged around his neck. Somehow, through sheer determination and possibly by torquing that great blocky head of his back and forth for hours, he'd wrestled himself free. He was a real warrior.

For my part, I certainly didn't grow up to be an animal enthusiast. In fact, I was downright terrified of dogs. Blame it on a traumatic encounter with a rogue Great Dane when I was a child. I was pedalling for dear life on my bike, with this massive dog running alongside me, matching my pace, barking furiously and showing far too much tooth for my liking. I always rode my bicycle everywhere and, on this day, I was on my way back from tennis coaching with Jenny Waggot, who had a tennis court in the garden of her lovely home in Pendennis Road, Mount Pleasant, an adjacent suburb to Groombridge.

I was convinced I was about to be mauled. My tennis racquet was strapped to the saddle at the back of my bike, completely useless in that moment. I didn't fancy stopping to negotiate with this dog, nostrils flaring and baring his teeth. Thankfully, the road turned downhill, and then gravity and sheer terror did the rest. With my heart pounding and crying wildly, I managed to make it home. I collapsed in a heap, with an even more profound fear of dogs.

Looking back, my fear probably had deeper roots. Mum had been badly bitten on the face by a neighbour's dog when she was only four. Innocently, she had gone to pat the dog through the fence, unaware that food time was not the time to be near any animal. The dog wasn't interested in being petted and, defending its meal, attacked her. The entire side of her face, through her nose and lips, was ripped open. Her skin was hanging loose off her face and, thankfully, she closely missed having her eyes gouged by the dog's claws.

It had left her with scars, both physical and emotional, and a lifelong distrust of dogs, no matter how small or well-behaved they appeared. She had recounted the story many times, and her fear became my fear. That moment on my bicycle, I was imagining myself in my mum's position.

Still, despite my nervousness, Obos won me over. Sadly, he passed away some years later from a tumour. Johnny was heartbroken. That dog had been his shadow, his protector, his gentle beast and best friend.

Johnny always had a thing for dogs. Not just owning them but also training them. He had taught his first dog, 'Lassey', to walk around the edge of his new lounge carpet. No paws or shoes were allowed on the fluffy stuff. Guests too had to remove their shoes at the door. When I came on the scene, and Lassey had sadly died, the rules around dogs were changed. The new dogs were not allowed into the living areas, and guests could keep their shoes on!

Over the years, we had several litters of puppies from our beautiful Bullmastiffs, Boris and Tasha. They were magnificent dogs with the gentlest of natures. Tasha was a wonderful mother, and the kids absolutely adored those little puppies. They would spend hours sitting beside the big wooden box, giggling as the little bundles of wrinkled skin tried to clamber over the edge, their curious noses poking everywhere. It was impossible not to fall in love with every single one of them, and it was always a sad day when they went off to their new homes.

I digress, so forgive that doggy diversion, and let's get back to Australia and Perth in particular, which had already been woven quietly into the fabric of Johnny's story, long before it became part of 'our story.'

He used to say, even back then, 'If I ever leave Zim, it'll be for Perth' – and he meant it.

But before reaching that chapter of our life, we had to face one small hitch. Those elusive documents. As it turns out, you do need proper paperwork to get married. A birth certificate for starters and, of course, the Catholic church requires a Baptism certificate too. Having your name typed in a passport with a birthplace that says Liverpool simply doesn't quite cut it!

5

Life-Changing Letter

So, there we were, standing in the Portuguese Embassy in Harare. I figured that, surely, we would be able to find out something about Johnny's arrival in Salisbury (now Harare). We had come hoping to chase down his birth certificate, immigration records, travel documents or anything official.

Johnny had forgotten much of his Portuguese, since he hadn't spoken it for many years, and explaining our queries to the lady at the counter was proving difficult, to say the least. However, we did manage to get some information. There were records of Johnny's father, José Berenguer, and Johnny's older brother, also named José, but nothing at all for Johnny. There was a spelling difference in the surname... this was our first realisation that there would be issues to follow. We didn't know then how much our lives would be affected by that spelling difference. We couldn't understand. How could the two of them be there in the records, but not Johnny? It was very strange indeed... as if he didn't exist!

Then, as if brought there by divine timing, a woman walked in. She spoke both Portuguese and English and we began chatting. I explained to her why we were there. Then, as fate would have it, she told us that the reason she was getting a visa was because she was traveling to Madeira Island. Not just anywhere in Madeira, but unbelievably she was going to Machico, Johnny's hometown.

We were stunned. What were the chances?

I told her about our challenges in finding information about Johnny, and our predicament due to our pending marriage. Not only did she offer to help translate to the consulate our problem in more detail, but she then went one step further. She offered to try to find Johnny's family while in Machico and gather any documents or information that could help us. I found a piece of paper and quickly wrote a letter for her to deliver on our behalf. Her name, sadly, escapes me now (I'm usually very good with names) so, let's just call her Maria.

Some people might call it a coincidence. I call it God's hand at work.

We waited anxiously for Maria's return from the Island. To be honest, I wasn't holding out much hope that she'd manage to dig up anything about Johnny's Madeiran roots. However, about a month later, word came back, and oh my goodness, what a surprise it was! Not only had Maria somehow tracked down Johnny's family home, but, by pure chance, or divine timing, as I like to think, his father happened to be there. Apparently, he quite frequently travelled between Madeira and South Africa, where he now lived and ran a little shop. He just happened to be visiting home when Maria knocked on the door. Honestly, what are the odds?

But it gets even better. Maria didn't come back with only news, she brought treasures too! She'd managed to get Johnny's original birth and baptism certificates, and most incredibly, a handwritten letter from his father. Unbelievable! That letter was both beautiful and heartbreaking.

The words in almost illegible handwriting on that note, in very basic Portuguese, explained that the family had believed Johnny had died after disappearing all those years ago. They were in absolute disbelief to hear he was alive and well. His father said he was now living in South Africa, in a place called Waterval Boven, and invited us to visit him at the address he'd included, when he returned in a month's time.

That scrappy and hurriedly written little note, which I had sent with Maria, had somehow opened a door to a whole new chapter. Johnny had found his father! We might even have the chance to meet his family. What an unexpected, wonderful turn of events!

Immediately, we made plans to travel down to South Africa to meet him.

The build-up to that trip was almost unbearable. The nerves, the curiosity and the deep, old heartache all swirling under the surface. As we drove toward Waterval

LIFE-CHANGING LETTER

Boven, the kilometres slowly adding up on the clock, the air in the car was thick with unspoken questions. What would he look like now? Would Johnny even recognise him? What if he didn't? What if it all went horribly wrong?

We were engaged by then, planning a future together, but this part, this unresolved, shadowy chapter of Johnny's past, hovered just beyond the edges of our story. I knew little bits and pieces, just not the full picture. Not yet.

As we pulled into the that little town over the bridge (the town's name came from its position above the waterfall) and parked in the road outside the shop, I could feel my heart pounding. Mine, and Johnny's too, though he seemed to be able to hide it. Sixteen years had passed. Sixteen long years since he'd last seen his father. Sixteen years of silence, of suppressed anger, of unhealed wounds, and a boy's promise to never look back. He had completely disassociated himself from his Portuguese heritage.

And then we walked through that door.

It was instant and it was incredible. I couldn't believe what I was witnessing. Johnny saw him. Recognised him. There was no hesitation, nor any dramatic pause. Johnny just rushed forward as though his feet had made the decision before his brain could do so. He wrapped his arms around his father, and the years crumbled away. There were tears, real, heaving sobs that came from both of them, and from me. They clung to each other like two halves of something that had been broken, trying to fit together again.

I stood there, barely breathing. It was surreal, as though I was watching a film scene. One that I didn't realise I was a part of. I didn't know then, what I would come to learn over the next few days. About the violence, the drinking, and the unimaginable trauma. About how Johnny had once run for his life, literally, from this very man. About how he had sworn he'd never see him again. About how, at one point, his father had even tried to kill him. It was mind-blowing!

But somehow, in that instant, none of that stood between them.

Forgiveness, when it arrives, is both strange and powerful. It doesn't always come with logic. Sometimes it just rises up. And that moment, so very raw and heartbreaking and at the same time so beautiful, will be seared into my memory forever. I can still close my eyes and see them embracing each other.

Then, with the tears still fresh between Johnny and his father, came the next incredible shock.

Standing there, was a woman, wiping at her eyes with the back of her hand, clearly overcome. She stepped forward and joined in the hug with such emotion, that I instinctively assumed this must be Johnny's long-lost mother. But no! This was not his mother at all. I was to discover that this was his aunt, Tia Katarina! His aunt and now also somehow his stepmother! There was a sweet little girl looking on, her hair in long dark plaits. She was Anna, their daughter. She was about four or five years old, wide-eyed and wanting to join in on the hugs.

It was, well… totally wild. Johnny had found his father and at the same time, discovered he had a sister who also happened to be his cousin. From that moment on, the week became a whirlwind of stories. Of fitting puzzle pieces into place (some upside down), and there were rivers of tears. Some of those tears were healing, some were just sad. It was a great deal to take in. It was emotionally overwhelming and sometimes it felt completely surreal.

Johnny's father, as it turned out, hadn't changed all that much, from his early Rhodesia[1] (Zimbabwe) days. Still a big drinker, still with a temper simmering just under the surface. There seemed to be a shadowed look in his eyes, and a kind of sadness about him. He was polite, but hard. He rarely seemed to smile. To be completely honest, I was rather afraid of him. I watched Johnny with quiet awe at the way he was able to sit there, listening and absorbing. He never flinched and never raised his voice. There were no accusations, nor any judgment. He just gracefully listened to Tia and his dad. With that gentle, cheeky humour of his, he somehow made even the most unbearable moment feel a little more manageable.

Some evenings were completely detached from the present unfolding situation, as they both sat in the small lounge, watching rugby, of all things, on the TV. The comments between them, for that brief time, were as if this father and son had never been apart. I remember how his father laughingly described that what he was in fact watching, was a herd of sheep! The big players grunting and following each other round the field!

---

1. On December 12th, 1979, Rhodesia ended its colonial rule and became the nation of Zimbabwe.

It amazed me. This extraordinary clashing of characters, in some ways similar but mostly completely opposite.

As the stories unfolded, we pieced together what had happened after Johnny had been taken from Madeira to Rhodesia. His mother, Filomena, had later also left Madeira for Venezuela, following Laurinda, Johnny's older sister. Laurinda married in Venezuela, and later Antonio, the youngest brother, followed with his mother. All Johnny's memories of his siblings were beginning to make their way back into his mind.

The family had become scattered, and over time, it seemed that bitterness had cemented the divide. The Venezuelan side of the family appeared to want nothing to do with Johnny's dad. They were weary of him and had been hurt deeply by him, especially after he'd married Filomena's own sister, Katarina. Apparently, whenever they travelled back to Machico, tongues would start wagging. There was tension and there was jealousy, and many whispered accusations. It had been safer, for many of them, to remain on opposite sides of the world.

No one seemed to know where exactly Filomena, Laurinda, or Antonio were living at that time. They knew only that they were somewhere in Venezuela, lost in time and distance. I felt a desperation to make this family come together. I remember thinking, as I stood there in that kitchen full of unfinished stories in Waterval Boven, 'We have to find them for Johnny's sake, and for closure.'

Eventually we did, but not for another twenty-three years. By then it would have been a total of thirty-nine years since Johnny had last seen them. How unbelievable, that it finally happened!

We learned that it had been José, Johnny's older brother, who had been the one tasked with finding Johnny all those years ago, when he had first disappeared.

In much the same way that Johnny had been brought out to Rhodesia, José too, had made that journey about four or five years earlier. He'd come to help their father with the shops, and in a way paved a path for Johnny to follow.

José was now living in Bophuthatswana, married with two sons at the time. He was managing some of his own shops there. He was not living in South Africa then because of the Apartheid government; his wife was of mixed race. We tracked him down and managed to contact him by phone. We tried to stay in touch, but it was very sporadic. The conversations were difficult and strained, always clouded by the blur of alcohol and pain. Truth and memory were hard to separate, and the details were all tangled together like vines. He told Johnny that he'd seen it all as a child growing up in Madeira, and he had witnessed his father's infidelities. That their father was secretly in love with Tia Katarina, even while married to their mother, Filomena. It had left deep scars in José. That betrayal had hurt him profoundly and caused him to distance himself from his father and Tia Katarina. This pain was probably the cause of his drinking and the many health challenges he complained about, whether real or imagined.

During our stay, I got a clearer picture of Johnny's father. A man of few words and many secrets. He certainly didn't suffer fools. Beneath his trousers, he had a pistol strapped to one leg under his sock, and a knife under the other! Yes, seriously! And he casually mentioned how he'd used his weapons more than once. My fear of this man grew. I couldn't help wondering whether those weapons may have been behind his reason for leaving Rhodesia, and why later, he left Mozambique. After all, you don't just keep skipping countries, unless you have a good reason, or maybe a few bad ones.

And, oh my word, those terrifying journeys with him to the wholesalers, to purchase stock for the store. We would pile into the front of the bakkie (South African term for a small pickup truck), Johnny's dad gripping the wheel like a man possessed. I'd be squashed between Johnny and his dad, holding on for dear life as we hurtled down the road at breakneck speed. I'm not exaggerating when I say I thought we might die. Multiple times. I was quietly saying my prayers, as if they were the last of my life.

We made it through that visit. Changed, most definitely. Moved, certainly. Confused, often. But mostly, I came away even more in awe of Johnny. The way he faced the pain and madness of his past, without letting it poison his future. It was humbling to witness his absolute forgiveness.

Of course, the story wasn't finished. Not by a long shot.

6

Sisters

Back in those early Madeira days, José Senior, Johnny's dad, had been something of a charmer in Ribeira Grande, the little village in Machico where they lived. He was handsome and popular; the centre of attention, the one that all the girls flirted with. He liked his drink, Cervaja (beer), or home-brewed Madeira wine or, even better, a strong pour of Aguardente (literally translated as 'fire water' and distilled from sugarcane). However, back in those days, love didn't always get a say. Marriages were often arranged, sometimes decided across tables and whispered in kitchens. Despite his heart belonging to Katarina, José was hurriedly married off to Filomena. Rumour has it that she was already expecting his child.

From there, things became very messy. There were infidelities and frequent shouting matches. Fists and fear tangled up with far too much alcohol. The discipline in the house wasn't discipline; it was fear. Johnny remembers some of those traumatic years, although he'd mostly tried to blot them out. Divorce back then simply was not an option in Catholic Madeira. You stayed, and you endured. And you didn't talk, at least, not in public.

Eventually, José left Madeira behind. Opportunity had knocked, and he set off to build another life in Africa. Many Portuguese people had gone to Africa before him and established successful building and construction businesses or shops and supermarkets, and José decided to follow suit. First stop for José was Rhodesia as it was then known, then Mozambique and finally, South Africa. José had built up several shops in different areas in those countries, selling all types of groceries and staples to the local population. His shop also made various small meals for sale. 'Russian and chips' was a firm favourite. This consisted of a thick garlic, spiced sausage made with pork or beef meat, served with a pile of double-fried chips. They weren't crisp chips, rather, soft on the inside and slightly soggy on the outside. All drenched in salt and vinegar. A South African fast-food classic.

Then came the twist. José, his heart aching for Katarina, eventually returned to Madeira to fetch her and take her back to South Africa with him. Yes, Katarina, the woman he'd always loved, the sister of his wife Filomena! They were married in South Africa, and together they had a child almost exactly nine months later. Sweet little Anna, a beautiful girl, clever and wise beyond her years, spiced with a cute cheekiness. She was the fruit of their forbidden love. He was still legally married to Filomena in Madeira.

Despite the fresh start, the ghosts came with him. José's drinking didn't stop. His temper was still sharp, ready to spark at any moment. Poor Katarina and Anna bore the brunt of it with quiet suffering, behind closed doors. We only found out many years later, just how difficult life with José had been for them in South Africa.

We later learned that Johnny had three other siblings back in Machico: Antonio (another boy with the same name as Johnny's youngest brother!) who was stillborn; Ana, also similarly named, but with just one 'n', who sadly died in infancy; and little Coltita, who was clearly his father's favourite at the time. Johnny's father shared memories of these daughters through tears, one night. He told us how he'd carried little Coltita in his arms, rushing to find a doctor. But it was too late, and he didn't make it there in time. Tragically she had died on the way. That memory, of her tiny, fading breath, seemed to be the only thing that broke through his usual stoicism. For a moment, the hardness cracked, and we saw the grief in his broken heart.

Something shifted in Johnny whilst listening to all of this. A few hazy memories surfaced and snippets of time with his baby sister Coltita, maybe a laugh, maybe a doll or perhaps holding her little hand walking down the path. But like so many who've carried childhood trauma, the good memories had been buried under layers of pain and silence. Madeira, Machico, his Portuguese heritage, he'd rejected it all. He would physically remove himself if he heard people speaking the language. It was too close and still too raw, and too full of things that had once hurt. Even now, he gets cold shivers when he hears people speaking aggressively in Portuguese.

That visit was healing, yes, but it was also draining. Perhaps it was somewhat therapeutic in places, but there had been so many emotional landmines. Wounds had been opened wide, and dreams became stirred up with nightmares. It was all still very tangled.

But we left with something new: a chapter we never could have ever expected. Anna, his little sister and cousin, all in one! She was now a part of his story. A sweet surprise in the middle of all that sorrow.

We came home carrying everything. The grief and all the revelations, the many questions still unanswered, and a quiet kind of hope that maybe, just maybe, the pieces would slowly start to come together.

A few months later, we were married. The focus on wedding preparations and arrangements had taken the bulk of our attention after our trip to Waterval Boven. I couldn't believe how quickly the past year had unfolded, with all the strange twists and turns, and now suddenly, here I was, about to marry someone I never in my wildest dreams could have imagined I would.

We had a beautiful outdoor farm wedding on Forrester Estates F Section. Hans and Shirley Maartens and their team of helpers had kindly set it all up. A gorgeous little chapel had been erected in their beautiful garden for the Traditional Catholic nuptial Mass. We were surrounded by most of my family and many of our dear friends, and of course, the tennis buddies who had been part of our journey from the start. Mini MacDonald was not only a major part of the tennis scene, he was also closely connected to Johnny's Mvurwi life, and so naturally he was Johnny's best man at our wedding. He had always been, and still is, one of Johnny's best friends. He and his wife, Ant, became like family to us. There's a kind of bond that goes beyond just friendship, a deep connection that has lasted through all the years. And even though life eventually pulled us to opposite sides of the world, we've always stayed in touch across the oceans, and whenever we talk, it's as if no time at all has passed.

Our kids grew up together, running in and out of each other's homes and more often than not, our gatherings took place somewhere around a tennis court. Mini and Ant had always been an integral part of Johnny's story and, by extension, mine too.

The wedding was a joyous occasion and the whole district were happy to see Johhny and I married, as he had long been the confirmed bachelor of the area. It had been a whirlwind engagement, and it felt as though everything had happened in 'fast-forward'. It was extraordinary to think that I had met him at the one tennis festival and then returned the very next year with an engagement ring on my finger, and, as it happened, by the following year, the third consecutive Mvurwi tennis festival, I now had a wedding ring next to the engagement ring.

It was impossible for Johnny's dad, aunt, and half-sister to join us at the wedding, despite our pleading that they do so. However, his dad insisted we go to Madeira on honeymoon and as a very kind gesture he contributed towards the trip. We were now Mr and Mrs Berenger, English spelling: more on that later!

Another unexpected turn in this wild, wild story.

To truly understand Johnny, and the path that brought him to me, we have to go back much further in time.

You see, as I previously mentioned, in the minds of Johnny's family, he had been dead for over a decade!

On the traumatic night, when Johnny apparently disappeared from his family, his father had sent Johnny's older brother, José, to search for him. But José, cut from the same cloth as his father, always drinking and mixing with the wrong crowd, came back later with a chilling story – that Johnny had been killed in the bush war.

Whether he made it up or simply repeated a rumour, it became the truth, and the family clung to the story. The news spread to Madeira, where they mourned his death. Unbelievable! The family wore black for six months, as Portuguese tradition dictated.

Meanwhile, Johnny was very much alive, under care of the state, at St Joseph's House for Boys and was attending Prince Edward School.

But with Johnny 'gone,' so to speak, his brother José, clearly saw an opportunity. He began using Johnny's full Portuguese name for some rather shady dealings. Suddenly there were accusations of outstanding debts, goods having been purchased on credit and never settled, and all this had been done under Johnny's name. It had all come to light just before we were married, when we decided to formally change Johnny's name into the English version he was using, so that all the documents, such as bank accounts, passport and driver's licence, matched. What we didn't know was that when a name is legally changed, a notice is published in the newspaper. That little announcement resulted in a number of companies thinking they'd found their man.

What a problem!

Thankfully, the lawyer helped to get it all wiped clean. The evidence was clear that it hadn't been Johnny at all. These were the same alarming listings that had surfaced in my mother's background search. The very things that had cast so much suspicion on him.

As Johnny had no official documents when he arrived at the police station all those years ago, he seemed to have somehow assumed an English version of his name. Over time, as he adapted to life in Rhodesia, he simply became 'Johnny.' Johnny Berenger. That's the name of the man whom I had met. That's the name everyone knew and now knows him to be. But to his family in Machico, he had died as João Luis.

7

Unaccompanied

Now finally, it's time to tell you what really happened when Johnny supposedly 'died', as far as his family knew.

João Luis Franco Moniz, or Johnny, as he will always be to me, was born in 1959 on the island of Madeira. A place so breathtakingly beautiful it feels as if God must have spilled His paintbox over it, splashing colour in every shade across the volcanic cliffs, the lush valleys and the endless blue of the Atlantic Ocean.

Johnny's father was a very hardworking man. Though the family's roots could be traced back to France, generations of the family had long since blended into the rhythms of Madeiran life in Maroços, a village tucked into the town of Machico. Over the years, the family had acquired little pockets of land scattered in and around Maroços and Ribeira Grande. Life in the village was simple; families grew what they ate and lived mostly off the land.

Each morning before sunrise, José would lace up his worn shoes and set off on foot, walking miles into Machico town to fetch fresh bread from the bakery. Then he'd trek all the way back to Maroços, carrying the warm loaves, selling them to neighbours in their stone houses, tucked into the hillsides.

On the terraces carved into the mountain slopes, the family grew beans, cabbage, potatoes and grapevines. Higher up, their lands stretched along the ridges, scattered with sugarcane, apple, banana and plum trees, and almost every fruit and vegetable you could imagine. It was a humble life, built on endless hours of hard work. Wine and Aguardente were everyday staples. Johnny's father never started a morning without tipping a little of that 'fire water' into his coffee. Meals often came with *'bolo do caco,'* delicious, soft Madeiran flatbread made with sweet potatoes, lovingly baked in their earth ovens. Every home had one of these.

Everywhere you turned there were little coffee shops and bars at the foot of the terraced homes. What struck me deeply when I met Johnny's aunt, Tia Katarina, was that the only thing she could write was her name. She had learned to just do that, for official papers, nothing more. She couldn't read at all, nor could Johnny's mother. Many women of that generation had little or no schooling.

Life was travelled on foot in those days, and fitness wasn't an option, it was survival. To get to the farmlands you needed to climb the steep mountainsides, following along narrow paths edged by stone walls, neatly stacked rocks without a drop of cement between them. This kept the soil from sliding away down into the river valleys miles below.

The roads connecting Machico and the little towns along the way to Funchal, the capital, were thin ribbons of tar clinging to cliff edges, twisting and turning like a coiled snake. Buses rattled along them, hugging waterfalls and plunging into tunnels carved through the volcanic rock. Drivers would hoot before every blind bend, sometimes inching past each other with just a whisper of space to spare. There were no long, straight highways like we know here in Australia, just endless hairpin bends and spirals wrapping around the wild terrain. Today, enormous modern tunnels cut through the mountains, shortening the distance, but Johnny still remembers being wide-eyed as a boy, dreaming of becoming a bus driver. He admired those men who could navigate such impossible roads with nothing but a steady hand and a blaring horn.

As a child in Maroços, Johnny's days were filled with chores, fetching firewood, carrying water, feeding the pig, splashing about in the river, and then racing off when the family's turn came to collect water from the canal. The *'levada'* runs all the way from the mountain top, snaking down past terraced houses to the valleys. Each family was allotted a time to draw off water from the levada for their land. Johnny would climb to their spot, as soon as the whistle was blown, and let the water irrigate the lands, fill his buckets, and carefully make the descent home, every step a balancing act so as not to spill a drop. That water was for drinking, or used for cooking, cleaning and bathing. Back then, there was no electricity or running water in any of the village homes.

There was a little school down the hill, and the children walked there each day. After classes, they played soccer or traditional games like '*jogo da macaca*' (hopscotch). One of Johnny's favourites was a rustic mix of cricket and baseball, nothing fancy, just a stick to whack a stone as far as you could. And when they weren't working or playing games, the kids simply got up to mischief, as children everywhere do.

Johnny was just twelve years old when he left Madeira for Rhodesia. I can't begin to imagine what that must have been like. Leaving behind the familiar comfort of the mountains, the salty sea air, his family and everything that had shaped his childhood, to go to a completely unknown place, where people spoke a language he could not understand.

I think about our son, Antonio, who, at the time of writing this, was a similar age to Johnny's then. I honestly can't imagine him having to experience something like that. How would he cope? But somehow Johnny did. He went obediently and quietly, without fuss, and certainly with a kind of bravery that only makes sense when looking back years later. An unbelievable strength and an unspoken courage. Not all heroes wear capes. Some of them are twelve-year-old boys doing what needs to be done.

When Johnny arrived in Rhodesia, he had no official documentation. It seems as if his father had never registered him, or perhaps he had not done it correctly, so that Johnny somehow slipped through the cracks. The first real trace of Johnny appears at St. Joseph's House for Boys in Salisbury (Harare).

It appears that Johnny entered the country with no passport, no birth certificate, just a name and a story. If there had been any documentation, it was lost somewhere along the way. He remembers being on the aeroplane with a lady, a family friend of sorts, I suppose. And then suddenly he arrived into a whole new world!

As a mother myself, I can't begin to imagine what that parting must have felt like for Filomena. She knew her husband's temperament, of course, but I think in her heart she must have believed Johnny would truly have a better life in Rhodesia. And maybe, just maybe, she didn't want to stir José's temper by resisting. So, she accepted it and let Johnny go. But I wonder if she realised then, that she might never see her little boy again? That thought makes my heart stop every time.

As Johnny's mother couldn't read or write, there were never going to be any letters written to him, and any correspondence from Johnny would have had to be read aloud to her. In today's world of instant texts and video calls, it's almost impossible to wrap our heads around that kind of silence and distance.

But that was the reality. A young boy, far away from home, carrying nothing but his name and the fading memories of where he came from. Memories he would soon try to forget, as I came to understand.

Johnny lived with his dad, José, in a small house perched just above their store on 51 Charter Road in Salisbury. José junior, his brother, ran another shop not too far away, so between them the family was busy with running multiple stores. In those days, many entrepreneurial Portuguese families, from Madeira, Mozambique, Angola and other Portuguese-speaking corners of the world, had made their way to Rhodesia. They opened little shops, supermarkets and construction companies. Before long, these grew into thriving businesses that kept whole communities ticking along.

However, José senior was hardly ever around, always doing things elsewhere, so Johnny ended up spending most of his days in the shop, alone with the staff. The African women who worked there took him under their wing, watching out for him as if he were their own. He swept the floors and stacked the shelves, he served customers from behind the counter, just quietly doing what needed doing, day after day.

The shop sold cigarettes too, rows and rows of every brand you could think of, neatly lined up on the shelves. It didn't take long before little Johnny became curious. Somewhere along the line, either encouraged by the staff or just imitating what he saw the grown-ups and customers doing, he picked up the habit of smoking. Hard to believe, but by the age of thirteen he was well and truly hooked. A chain-smoking youngster! The very thought still shocks me.

The shop staff would share their cigarettes with him without a thought, and he would puff away as if it were the most normal thing in the world.

One day, he took it too far. He smoked a whole packet of Peter Stuyvesant, his brand of choice. The entire pack was gone in one sitting! This was neither a wise nor a healthy decision and unsurprisingly, he ended up horribly sick. He vowed, then and there, never to smoke another cigarette again. With that, he grabbed the rest of the carton and snapped every single cigarette into tiny pieces. From that day on, he never smoked again. I can't imagine a child of his age having the resolve to do that!

When people ask him at parties or gatherings whether he smokes, he loves to grin and say, 'Oh no, I gave up when I was thirteen.' Of course, no one ever believes him, and certainly the first time I heard him announce this, I didn't either, it sounded completely ridiculous. But the truth is, it's exactly what happened.

The hard shop routine began as soon as the door opened at first light and then ended only after the last sale was done. Sometimes this was late into the night. Johnny then went to sleep in their cramped little house, if you could call it that, just above the shop. A lot of the noise and chaos from the street below, could be heard.

I remember one day, out of curiosity, I drove past this very shop where Johnny had lived and worked as a boy. By then, it had become a butcher of sorts, called 'Kappies Meat Market.' It was a run-down and grubby-looking building when I saw it. It felt impossible to picture Johnny living there as a child, in this dodgy part of town.

There was no schooling. Johnny had never been enrolled. He simply worked in the shop, day in and day out. And then there was his father; mostly drunk, often angry, and rarely around except when he came back from socialising with the locals, usually in a foul mood. These dysfunctional circumstances were appalling for such a young boy to have to experience, but that was the only life he knew.

Then came the traumatic event, sometime in October 1972, a night that would change everything. Thieves broke into the shop and demanded all the money. Johnny, barely more than a boy and scared out of his wits, handed over the day's takings and everything in the till without hesitation. When his dad came back and found the cash drawer empty, he completely lost his temper. Drunk, furious and blinded by rage, he pulled out the knife that he always kept tucked in his sock and went for Johnny. Absolute chaos ensued. The maid, screaming and desperate, threw herself between them, and miraculously stopped the attack. I believe that her act of bravery saved Johnny's life that night.

Johnny fled, screaming down the dark streets. He remembered that the police station was only a few blocks away and so he ran there as fast as he could. When he got there, he blurted out what had happened, but he couldn't make himself understood, because he was able to speak only Shona and Portuguese. The officers had to bring in an African constable to translate his desperate sobs. Once they understood the situation, they decided that it simply wasn't safe for him to return to his father. In any case, Johnny had refused to go back; life with his dad had been utterly dismal. That was the last time he saw his dad until I came into his life.

The social welfare department was contacted, and they stepped in to manage what was clearly a sad and desperate situation. Johnny was placed at St. Joseph's House for Boys, an orphanage in Salisbury. It was there, at last, that life began to take on some kind of 'normal' for him, with structure, safety and the chance for a proper formal education. The boys from the home were sent to local schools: Selbourne Routledge for their junior years, and then later, either Allan Wilson or Prince Edward for high school.

8

Johnny Nonsense

The desperate act of courage that night of the robbery by a scared little boy, lost in a foreign land, running into the darkness for help, turned his life around.

Life at St. Joseph's House for Boys followed a steady rhythm. Each weekday morning began the same way. After breakfast, the boys would wash, dress and finish their chores before setting off on the walk to Prince Edward School, where Johnny had ended up. St. Joseph's House, affectionately known among the street kids as '*the joint*,' ran on structure and routine. It was almost regimental, but within that order, the boys learned discipline, and for Johnny, a sense of stability he'd never known before.

Johnny began to find his footing at PE, though schoolwork didn't come easily. He'd missed so many crucial years of foundational learning and it was an added difficulty, now having all lessons in what was not his native language. He already knew Shona from his days working in his father's shop, chatting with the African staff and picking up their turns of phrase and, no doubt, the odd swear word too. That same easy adaptability helped him, as he learned to joke, tease and charm his way through almost any situation.

Humour became his bridge and whenever the African staff, who had become his translators, came around with instructions, Johnny would whisper cheeky remarks like, 'Tell him he's got a big nose,' or 'Tell the cook his stomach's getting too big.' The staff and boys alike would burst out laughing. His quick wit, mischievous grin and knack for lightening any situation made him instantly likeable. He was speaking a jumble of Shona, Portuguese and newly learned English, but somehow everyone understood him.

Johnny's humour, I think, was more than mere entertainment. It was his means of survival, keeping him connected to the group around him. It was, and still is, his greatest gift.

Johnny tells of a time, with a twinkle in his eye, when as a prefect on dinner table duty, he used to inspect the water spills under each boy's cup. Then he would measure the size of the puddle and charge them according to the matching-sized coin. I'm not sure if this was an early sign of his budding business acumen or simply 'dinnertime robbery', but it seemed to become common practice, and consequently 'table prefect' became the most desired position in the dining hall. And... the kids learned not to be clumsy at the table!

During his years at Prince Edward, Johnny made many friends; bonds that lasted well beyond those school years. One of these friends was Mini, who proudly stood beside Johnny as best man at our wedding. Mini often laughs when he fondly recalls PE school days, describing Johnny as a bit of a 'Momparra'; a Shona word to describe a cheeky troublemaker who was always up to mischief.

His knack for using humour, wit and charm, and that trademark grin, nearly always allowed him to wriggle out of anything, including having to perform prefect initiations or dreaded tasks that he was assigned.

As often happened at St. Joseph's House for Boys, there were kind families that offered to take one or more of the boys into their home during the school holidays. The goal was simply to give the children a glimpse into ordinary family life. Something warm and gentle, a welcome contrast to the institutional routine they were used to.

It was during one of these holiday periods that a compassionate couple, Fred and Julie Botha, felt moved to open their home to a vulnerable boy. Fred and Julie, with two young daughters at the time, approached the orphanage and asked if there was any child in need of a place to stay during the school break. As fate would have it, that boy turned out to be Johnny.

From the moment he entered the Botha home, Johnny was treated like one of their own. It was as if he had stepped into another world, with the smell of home-cooked food in the kitchen, giggling and laughter from the girls, and soft embracing hugs from Julie and Fred as they tucked him in at night. This life was so very foreign to him. Fred and Julie gave him gentle structure, always with kindness and patience. Their kids welcomed him as a brother, and for the first time in years, Johnny felt what family was meant to be like; special moments that have shaped him.

Most school holidays were spent just being a teen, riding bikes with the other Botha kids, swimming in Fred's parents' pool, and playing in the yard until the sun went down. For once, life wasn't about survival or fear, it was about fun, noise and laughter. He finally was able to experience those ordinary, everyday moments of childhood that are often taken for granted. He now had a strong, steady father figure in Fred, who, having always been somewhat outnumbered by females in his family, absolutely loved having another male around the house.

Fred had finally found someone to teach and share 'boy' things with; how to shoot a gun and how to drive the homemade buggy. And he could also just quietly be there for Johnny, when it was needed. Julie still laughs when she tells the story of the first time Johnny fired a rifle. The recoil flung him flat onto his backside, with a rather impressive bruise shining on his shoulder as proof of the adventure.

She remembers that when Johnny first arrived, he was extremely quiet. He didn't speak much, and when he did, it was in Shona. However, that didn't last long, as he was soon confidently speaking both English and Shona languages, and talking and playing with the kids. He kept his past to himself, but they quickly noticed his sense of humour and natural charm as he slotted into the family.

Of course, it wasn't all sunshine and innocence. Johnny had a mischievous streak, a stubborn sparkle that did sometimes land him in trouble. During one of the school breaks, while the Botha family was staying on Empress Nickel Mine where Fred was working, Johnny got up to what became a legendary story in the family.

Without permission, and of course, without really knowing how to drive, Johnny decided it would be a brilliant idea to go fishing and that he should take the farm truck to get there. After all, Fred had shown him how to 'drive' in the buggy. Unsurprisingly, the adventure ended in complete disaster when he lost control of the truck whilst negotiating a sharp bend on a downward sloping, dirt road. He flipped the truck, resulting in it being declared a total 'write-off.' Johnny ended up in hospital for a brief time, but thankfully, his injuries were minor.

Fred was understandably furious, but in true Botha style, he and Julie forgave him and welcomed him back for the next school holidays. That act of grace spoke volumes.

They saw past the mistake and into the wounded boy who was simply trying to experience a little freedom. It was unusual for the orphans to go on holiday breaks with always the same family. They were normally swapped around with all the host families. However, in Johnny's case, the Botha family requested to have Johnny on an ongoing basis. A special bond had grown between them.

Decades passed and life moved on. But sometimes, God weaves unexpected moments of restoration into the fabric of our lives.

Through the marvel of Facebook, Fred and Julie's eldest daughter, Janine, found me. She had been searching for Johnny for some time. She reached out with a message, hoping to somehow reconnect with him. I couldn't believe that, after so many years, this family, who had been so incredibly kind and had made such a difference in Johnny's life, should suddenly re-emerge. We exchanged details, then we exchanged memories, and I even managed to see a few photos. These are the only photos I had ever seen of him as a teenager. The resemblance to our own kids is uncanny. Eventually, as a result of this Facebook discovery, we reconnected with Julie herself. It was truly incredible.

Sadly, we learned that Fred had passed away in 2016. Even more heartbreaking was the news that Janine had died in 2021 from COVID, a loss we hadn't known about until later. We were overjoyed when, in 2023, a reunion was made possible. Julie and her sisters met in Perth for a long-awaited family gathering to celebrate a milestone birthday. One of her sisters lives here in Western Australia, and this visit gave us the chance to see Julie and for her and Johnny to meet in person once more.

After nearly fifty years, half a century, they were reunited. It was an emotional and unforgettable moment. There were hugs, there were tears, and a flood of stories from a different lifetime. Julie said it best:

'He was a fun-loving boy, always up to mischief. But Fred and I couldn't stay angry for long. We knew what he'd been through. We gave him a pass, I suppose. What he really needed was a family, ... and we were lucky enough to be the ones to give that to him, even just for a while.'

Despite strict rules, and endless chores at 'the joint', Johnny as we discovered, always found relief in getting up to mischief.

Once a week, the boys from St Joseph's would head off to Boy Scouts at the hall just down the road from GHS (Girls High School). On one particular night, something far more memorable than knot-tying and Morse code unfolded.

The Scouts session had wrapped up, but instead of heading straight back to 'the joint', Johnny and a few of the boys felt like some fun. As they wandered past the GHS hostel, the glow of the dormitory lights and the sounds of teenage girls chattering and laughing drifted through the open windows. This was way too tempting for the boys.

There they were, windows open, moonlight reflecting off the drainpipes, practically inviting them in for an adventure. In a flash, and with the ease and stealth of small-time cat burglars, they had scaled the pipes and had slipped into the girls' dormitory like shadows.

At first, it was shrieking chaos, screams of fright, which then quickly turned into squeals of teenage glee as the girls soon realised it was just the naughty boys from St Joseph's dropping in for a surprise visit. Then there were screams and laughter – it was absolute mayhem. But it was glorious and exhilarating fun too, though all too short-lived.

The matron, sharp as a hawk and probably no stranger to these sorts of stunts, had heard the commotion and came thundering down the dormitory corridor, with all her matronly authority. The boys didn't wait around for her scolding. Out they flew, slipping down the drainpipes just as fast as they'd gone up, giggling breathlessly.

Back at St Joseph's, the boys told and retold the story until it became legend.

And so, 'the joint' was Johnny's life for a couple of years but, by the time he reached the age of fifteen, something had shifted. Johnny reckoned he needed a new direction. Most boys at that age don't make life-altering choices – however, he did.

He decided he should leave school and enlist in the Rhodesian Army, as the bush war was now raging in Rhodesia (now Zimbabwe). He knew it was dangerous, something in him felt drawn to serve, to find direction and purpose. So, without much hesitation, he set off toward a new chapter, determined to make sense of his life. He set out with nothing more than a small bag of clothes, determined to build a life worth living.

9

15 and Fearless

By 1975, Rhodesia was already consumed by the Bush War. Guerilla fighters had ambushed numerous roads, farms were constantly being attacked by 'terrorists,' villages were braced for reprisals, and nearly every able-bodied young man felt the pull of duty. Whether this was by choice or by compulsory call-up, they felt it. For a boy who'd already survived abandonment, violence and an orphanage, joining the Rhodesian Light Infantry wasn't simply an act of patriotism, it was a desperate grasp for purpose. So off Johnny went.

At the sign-up office, the sergeant asked for his birth certificate, and his documentation. He didn't have anything. There was not one piece of paper that said he existed beyond attending St. Joseph's House for Boys. Yet the sergeant looked at him, saw something in this young boy's eyes, a hunger, I guess, and it seems the form was somehow filled out, despite the lack of paperwork. Soldiers were desperately needed, in any case.

He was to report to Cranborne Barracks, home of the Rhodesian Light Infantry (RLI) along with a group of other recruits. Intakes were numbered according to the dates of sign-up. He was part of 'Intake 149'.

First stop was the barbers, as the boys had to have their hair cut short before being marched to the QM (Quartermaster), where they were measured up and issued all the basic requirements; uniforms, which included boots, trousers, and a jacket. Just like that, he was now officially in the Rhodesian Light Infantry battalion.

What followed was four months of RLI recruit training. A very tough course that drilled them in discipline, something he had already learned from 'the joint'. All the new recruits were taught weapons handling, tactics, and parade-ground drill. At the end of his training, Johnny was posted to Support Commando and although now a fully qualified soldier, he was just sixteen years old. A *'boy-soldier.'*

Johnny had successfully completed all the necessary training; the correct way to handle and fire the rifles, drills, tactical manoeuvres - he had learned everything. However, instead of being out in the bush where the real action took place, he found himself relegated to kitchen duty, peeling potatoes and washing dishes. It drove him mad. He hated being stuck there. He wasn't made for KP (kitchen patrol) duty; he was just itching to be in the thick of it with the other troopies.

One night, the base sirens went off, and everyone scrambled, grabbing their weapons and jumping into the '4-5s' - those rickety, open-backed military trucks. Without saying a word, Johnny had snuck in too. No one seemed to have noticed Johnny jump into the truck. The troopies assumed they were all accounted for, and off they went.

Then, mid-contact, a burst of gunfire rang out from a completely unexpected direction. For a moment, everyone thought they'd been flanked. 'Who the hell is that?' someone shouted over the chaos. A troopie was ducked behind cover and firing accurate and purposeful shots, as if he was a seasoned soldier. He was bloody brilliant. Turns out… it was Johnny.

Naturally, chaos followed. He was hauled in for questioning and put on military disciplinary orders. But it quickly became clear that he wasn't some reckless kid trying to play soldiers, he was the real deal. He was talented, focused and determined to contribute to, and be in on, the action.

A solution needed to be found, because if they didn't find a way to involve him officially, he'd probably keep sneaking out and joining in.

Enter Pat Armstrong; a major and the commander of Support Commando of the RLI. Whether it was divine intervention or perhaps a little strategic bullying from Padre Bill Blakeway, who always had a soft spot for Johnny, Pat, a bachelor and just twenty-seven at the time, begrudgingly agreed to take Johnny under his wing, officially, as his legal guardian. He agreed to do this only because he hugely respected Padre Bill, and by doing so, he became more than just Johnny's commanding officer. He became a mentor, a protector, and someone Johnny would regard with the utmost admiration for the rest of his life.

For the next three years, Johnny was in full-time service as a regular soldier.

Johnny often wished he could reconnect with Pat. Once he'd left the RLI, all contact had been lost. Quite coincidentally, or by Divine timing, a connection was recently made. They re-established contact, sharing phone calls and catching up on life after the army days.

Johnny was deeply grateful to have made this very special reconnection.

During those army years, Johnny would often spend his R&R (rest and recuperation) breaks with Tiens, Cindy and their family. They became like a second home to him, and it was a welcome escape from the tension of bush life. He'd met the family earlier, through contacts at the ice-skating rink.

Johnny had been introduced to ice skating while still at school, during his holiday stays with the Bothas. He proved to be a natural. Once on the ice, he would speed skate around the rink, pulling off impressive jumps and turns. He even helped instruct beginners.

I had no idea of this hidden talent of his until he nonchalantly mentioned it after we were married. I used to love going ice-skating, and after watching stars like 'Torvill and Dean' or the Olympic figure skating on TV, I imagined I was just like them. However, the reality was that there was more slipping and sliding than gliding. It was such a treat to spend an afternoon or evening on the ice as a child. Unfortunately, the rink closed down before we were married, so I never got to see him in his element.

Years later, when we were on holiday in South Africa, we did find a rink somewhere. Johnny stepped onto the ice, just for fun, and within moments I could see that he still had the ability to glide effortlessly across the ice. I could barely stay upright and made my way round the edge, unsteadily sliding whilst gripping the rubber railing.

There's a rink in Perth and though, as yet we've never visited there, it is on the list of places to go.

At the end of one of the RnR breaks in 1976, the biggest intake of recruits (Intake 150), was gathered at Salisbury train station, heading to Bulawayo. Johnny was also due to board that train as he was to attend a medics course, but he'd forgotten his books, and needed to return to collect them. They were running late when Cindy dropped him at the station, so he sprinted along the platform to catch the train, books under one arm, rifle slung over his shoulder, just managing to catch the train as it was chugging out from the station.

He grabbed onto the upright pole at one of the carriage's doors and jumped, just as the train jolted, whilst the engine was beginning to pick up speed. His foot slipped off the step, and in a split second, he was down and onto the tracks. Metal screeched, and several of the carriages were derailed. It was bedlam on the platform. The train had jumped off the tracks, and somehow, Johnny had caused this mayhem.

Cindy, hearing the long wail of the train's horn, came running back in a panic, unsure what on earth had happened. The station was in pandemonium. People shouting over each other, pointing at the tracks, yelling, *'There's his leg!' 'There's his arm!'* – although no one really seemed sure if what they were seeing was real, or whether it was their panic-fuelled imagination.

Cindy frantically asked what had happened, and someone casually muttered, 'Some stupid idiot jumped onto the tracks.' There was also a throwaway comment about his appearance. With Johnny's olive skin and the deep tan he'd earned from countless hours outdoors, Cindy knew instantly, and with a sickening certainty, that it had to be him. She cried out, 'Oh my goodness, that's my adopted son down there!'

The little old lady standing beside her overheard and promptly keeled over and fainted, completely overcome by the shock of it all.

It took a while before they managed to find Johnny. Miraculously, he was still alive, wedged under the platform and between the steam pipes. It was like something out of a movie. Two ambulances arrived that afternoon, one for Johnny and one for the poor old lady who'd fainted!

Later, they discovered the cause of the derailment – his rifle! It had not only derailed the train but had probably saved his life. His shirt was cleanly cut into three pieces. All the army doctors at the hospital, examining the shirt and his rifle (now bent at a perfect right angle) were unanimous: 'there was no way anyone should have survived that.' But Johnny did. It was just another one of those 'only-Johnny' moments that we have come to expect. He spent some time in hospital to mend fractures to his 4th and 5th vertebrae, and then, true to form, he was back in service as soon as he was allowed.

Clearly, his time wasn't up. God had more in store for him.

The incident made the front page of 'The Rhodesia Herald' the next morning. To this day we are still hopeful of eventually finding that article in the newspaper.

Maybe someone reading this will know of someone who remembers something. Do let us know, in that event!

By 1976, Johnny had become part of the world-renowned Fire Force operations – Rhodesia's version of rapid airborne reaction. The idea was to get there before the terrorists had a chance to scatter; it was called 'vertical envelopment' and it was very strategic.

Support Commando's variant on the vertical envelopment tactic was where ground troops would be carried directly to the target by Dakota where they then made static line parachute jumps. It was a slick (and terrifying) manoeuvre. Airstrips in the middle of nowhere, a company of men, and aircraft on standby, ready to launch at the first crackle of a report over the radio; an ambush, a farm attack, or a sighting. The Selous Scouts would be out there in the bush, camouflaged into the land like lizards, eyes on the enemy, feeding through the coordinates. Most of the time, there was not even a proper base, just a dusty little airstrip and a commando full of young men who weren't afraid of a bit of chaos.

Officially, Rhodesian para drops were done from about 500 feet above ground level. Sometimes they'd push it to 400 feet if absolutely necessary, but never lower than that. Not unless you had a death wish. Any lower, and the parachute might not deploy properly. It wasn't trees they were worried about, unless they were particularly thorny, it was the lack of airspace to let your chute open before gravity introduced you to the ground... hard.

Johnny, as a part of Support Commando, was the MAG gunner in the stick, and lugged the beast of a weapon, providing serious firepower when needed. The stick leader always carried a radio, which was a lifeline, enabling them to communicate not only to the other sticks scattered throughout the bush, but directly to the K-car circling above, which also carried the airborne commander. That real-time coordination was one of the main reasons Fireforce worked as fantastically well as it did.

During one particular operation, most likely in early '77, things took a dangerous turn, leaving a lasting memory in Johnny's mind. They'd been scrambled to intercept a group moving through rugged terrain. There were many kopjes, and thick bush with sudden drop-offs. The terrain had forced the Dakota to fly way lower than normal – not exactly a parachute jumper's dream. They were doing their usual static-line jump. 'The little tap was felt on your behind and you were off along the line and out the door of the plane.' Johnny vividly recalls.

Only problem? The altitude. He swears the pilot must've dipped well below 400 feet, because, as he put it, 'I could count the damn rocks on the ground as I left the plane that day.' Not a comforting thought or the kind of reassurance you want before flinging yourself out of an aircraft. There was barely a moment for the 'chutes to bloom before they were yanked tight and the troops hit the dirt.

There were a few broken ankles and legs that day, but miraculously, no fatalities. Johnny, true to form, landed unscathed. Not even a scratch. He always did seem to have a knack for walking away from near disasters, with another great story to tell!

Incidentally, RAR (Rhodesian African Rifles) holds the record for the lowest parachute jump ever – around 250 feet! Sadly, that one did end in fatalities. A grim reminder that what these young men were doing wasn't just gutsy, it was very dangerous.

Whilst on an operation guarding a waterhole on the Mozambique border, things turned very quickly from routine to nightmare. Troops had been doing reconnaissance; watching, counting and gaining what intel they could about the 'terrorists' in the area. Landmines had already been swept and cleared to open a way for Support Commando to move through. Everything was tense, as the troops moved cautiously, weapons ready, scanning the bush.

Finally, when all seemed still, they allowed themselves a breather. Just a few quiet bites from their rations, in the shade of some Msasa trees.

Suddenly, out of nowhere, there they were – not '*terrs*' but Frelimo, (Mozambique's Guerrilla army) who had walked straight into their position. Deafening gunfire suddenly shattered the silence, bullets tearing through the bush. All hell broke loose, and the troops scattered, everyone diving for cover and pulling back towards the rendezvous point. Johnny, the MAG gunner, strapped with five heavy belts of ammunition, together with his corporal alongside him, stayed back and provided cover fire so the others could pull out of the madness. The MAG hammered out bursts into the thick bush as they held the line.

Then came the moment that still makes my heart stop to imagine.

The firing lulled for a moment. There was silence, as if the enemy were shifting. So, Johnny and the corporal took their chance to move out of there. As Johnny went to grab all his gear, the MAG got snagged in the 'V' of a tree branch. It was wedged tight. He yanked and he twisted ... frantically. It just wouldn't budge, as every second seemed to stretch forever. The enemy was silent, but panic was rising and his heart pounded in his chest. At any moment, gunfire could erupt. He truly thought this might be his end.

By some miracle, the MAG finally came free, and in one motion, adrenalin flooding through his body, he hoisted the 30-odd kilos of gun and ammunition up into the air and ran, sprinting for his life through the bush. He had the massive gun held high above his head, with one arm, as if it was weightless. Running for dear life.

There was some reprieve, but it was short-lived.

They were ambushed again! The bush erupted with gunfire for a second time. Somehow, by grit or luck or by the grace of God, they made it through without a single casualty. They spent the next few days and nights lying low, sleeping in the scrub, totally exhausted, and their nerves were stretched thin. Every little leaf rustle or crack of a twig had them on edge. They hoped desperately that they wouldn't be discovered. Then finally, after an endless wait, they heard the thudding sound of the choppers, who'd come to rescue them. Airlift was the only way out of that nightmare. Relief, at last.

At some point later, Johnny moved across to Support Commando's Anti-Tank Troop, call sign 44, first under Lieutenant Dick Stent and later, Lieutenant Simon Willar. His time there was marked by countless skirmishes and more than a few close calls that could so easily have gone the other way.

Pat made sure Johnny was released the moment his three years of obligatory service were up. But shortly before he left, there'd been a contact in Mtoko, an area code-named 'Operation Hurricane'.

It was a brutal one. During the chaos, something completely and utterly devastating happened. Two young troopies were killed. Johnny's mate, Earl, was hit, eighteen rounds into his young body. Eighteen! That was his first and last contact. George Clarke, lying right beside Johnny, was also shot and killed. It was horrific. Pat Armstrong had been in the helicopter K Car gunship that day, and it was also his last contact in the commando, as he had been posted to Army HQ.

A tragedy like that doesn't pass out of your mind. You carry it. The horrific images. The sounds. The sheer helplessness. That kind of trauma doesn't pack up and leave, as you do when your service ends. It stays ... and it haunts.

10

Mountains of Love

The day after our wedding, we boarded a flight bound for Madeira Island. We had a short stopover in Lisbon for the night, and then Johnny would be going 'home.' This time, he would have a wife by his side. We were still riding the high of the wedding, swept up in the excitement, reliving the happy moments of the day before, and now we were filled with anticipation at the thought of visiting Johnny's birthplace of Maroços in Machico, and all of his family still living there.

Our stay in Lisbon was the first stop on this emotional journey, and it also marked the start of Johnny trying to remember his Portuguese. He hadn't spoken it in years. He had managed to get a few sentences out to the man sitting next to us on the plane, but it was very broken. Most of the time, what came out was a jumble of Shona, English and Portuguese, all rolled into one.

There were plenty of wild guesses and an added Portuguese lilt on words that definitely didn't belong in the sentence! All of it was interspersed with 'Ummmms' and classic hand gestures – as if that might somehow recall the word from thin air.

I have always maintained that whatever language you mainly speak as a teenager is the one that your brain stamps in your head. It becomes your thinking language and also creates the accent that is likely to stick. Obviously, schooling and life in a different country can shift things. Deep down, I believe that your adolescent voice never really leaves you.

The day finally arrived. We were on the TAP flight bound for Funchal. I was very nervous. I had never travelled overseas or flown in a plane further than from Harare to Bulawayo.

At the time, there were strict limitations on airlines, and TAP was one of the few allowed to land in Madeira. This was all thanks to its renowned runway. Not only being among some of the shortest in the world, but also due to the surrounding terrain. There are hills and steep cliffs right beside the island's airport, and the runway juts out into the sea.

Pilots had to circle the airport and make a visual approach. They would have to navigate a 180-degree right turn before lining up for a very short final approach. Often the wind plays a major role in landing decisions, and – depending on the day – planes have been seen to be blown to the right and quickly to the left as they make their approach, appearing as though a disaster is about to happen, with the plane almost at right angles to the landing strip. But somehow these experienced pilots manage to steady the plane at the crucial moment just as the tyres hit the runway.

Only ten years prior, a plane travelling from Brussels via Lisbon to Madeira had crashed. The aircraft had attempted to land in poor weather conditions. It had done a 'go-round' first. The plane had landed way too far along the 1600m runway and had plunged over a steep bank. The right wing tore off after striking a stone bridge, and then crashed onto a beach. The aircraft caught alight, and sadly 131 lives were lost of the 164 souls on board.

Thank goodness the internet was 'not a thing' in those days and there were only vague stories which I had heard muttered when I mentioned our upcoming honeymoon on the island. I only discovered the details of that crash landing years after returning from our honeymoon. Incidentally, there are 'YouTube' channels dedicated to live screening every flight that departs or lands at Madeira airport, capturing all the incidents in real time. I have seen some incredible footage of near misses and very challenging landings in very windy weather conditions.

Hearing all the talk of dangerously short runways and mountain crashes was far from comforting in my nervous state. At least the runway had been slightly extended, a mere 200 metres just the year before in 1986 – some consolation. I was desperately hoping that the pilot flying the plane today had undergone his required 'extra training' and was super-experienced for the task at hand.

The Madeira Island runway was extended again in 2000, and is presently 2,781m long, which is still a challenge for even the most experienced pilots, the A330 being the largest plane allowed to land there. This extension was an extremely difficult feat for the construction company, as it was nearly impossible to use landfill for the extension. Instead, hundreds of very high columns were constructed to support a platform extending out by more than 900m towards the ocean, above a shallow-water bay. Quite an incredible undertaking.

As we descended, I caught sight of it through the little aeroplane window; a tiny sliver of tarmac perched on the edge of the mountainside, jutting out into the sea. All through that flight, I had quietly whispered a few decades of the Rosary, praying not only for a safe landing but also for a happy and meaningful honeymoon trip ahead.

The view we were met with was breathtaking. Lush green mountains, deep blue sea, little A-frame houses dotting the hillsides, and row upon row of banana plantations. I wasn't sure what I'd imagined Madeira would look like, but it certainly wasn't this. The island was simply stunning.

We had survived... and landed safely. Every person on the flight was clapping and cheering loudly. My eyes had been firmly closed from before touchdown until the plane was moving slowly towards the gate. I discovered that the clapping is a common occurrence on flights in Portugal and on Madeira Island specifically. The pilots absolutely need to be congratulated on landing their planes safely and without incident in those crazy airfield conditions.

At the airport, we were met by Johnny's aunt and uncle, Tia Conceição and Tio Joao. Incredibly, they recognised him immediately, and he recognised them too. It was a beautiful reunion to witness the warm hugs, the emotional tears and a flurry of Portuguese that was completely incomprehensible to me. They seemed to speak in a specific dialect, very quickly, and the more excited they became, the faster they seemed to speak!

The first few days passed in a blur as we were introduced to more and more family, each one expressing disbelief as they took in the sight of Johnny, not as the twelve-year-old João Luis who had left so long ago, but now a married man – changed yet familiar.

Every time we walked up the mountain roads, someone would stop us in delight, calling out, '*João Luís, João Luís, it's you!*' Word had spread through Maroços and Ribeira Grande that Johnny had returned. It was a small village where everyone knew everyone and faces weren't forgotten, so to see him suddenly appear 'alive' was a wonderful shock. Besides, Johnny's anticipated visit had been discussed in nearly every neighbouring household.

His father had built a beautiful and grand home on one of his wife's family's plots, in Ribeira Grande, down from Maroços, right next to the church. The church was also actually built on what used to be their property. His aunt and uncle lived immediately next door, and their homes were partially connected, sharing a garage below and a staircase that led across both houses.

Parked in the garage was a shiny Mercedes-Benz, proudly owned by Johnny's father. We were told we could stay in the house and use the car.

Driving on the island was a huge challenge, as the car had been sent over from Africa and was right-hand drive, in a country with predominantly left-hand drive cars. Poor Johnny had to adjust quickly, not only to driving on the 'wrong' side of the road, but also to the dizzying hairpin bends of the narrow, steep roads. It was wild, and we had several very near misses.

The house seemed to climb with the mountain, three levels rising with the slope. On the top floor, tucked in a corner, was a little room where a pig lived happily munching on kitchen scraps. Religious statues were everywhere, Jesus and the Virgin Mary placed lovingly in wall niches, and traditional ceramic tile panels depicting sacred scenes around the doorways. Flowerpots spilled over railings and terraces. Every spare inch of land was cultivated – vines, potatoes, sugar cane, some patches no bigger than a couple of metres but still bursting with life.

It was a scene full of colour, faith, family, and an overwhelming sense of connection. A homecoming in every sense of the word. It was truly amazing to see how at home Johnny seemed to be in their company, even though it was a long time since he had been there. He kept saying that everything had changed. He'd not been around to see the developments, the new houses, now complete with running water and electricity.

Our trip happened to be right in the middle of a Catholic feast in honour of the Virgin Mary, and – oh my goodness – what a sight to behold! All the little winding roads were strung with the most beautiful floral garlands, draped from rooftop to rooftop like something out of a fairy tale, all leading straight to the church. A huge statue of Our Lady was being carried on a bier in a glorious procession, right through the heart of the village. And where were we for all this? Right on the best balcony in town, Johnny's father's house, perched above it all with a front-row view of the whole celebration. It was magic.

One of our first little adventures was walking just down the road from Ribeira Grande and up the side of the hill, to see Johnny's old family home in Maroços. Clearly visible from the new house, it was perched up amongst the green of the mountainside.

It was hard to believe, but as we walked, Johnny started remembering names, places, and details, as if no time had passed at all. He pointed out where the schoolroom had been, the old shop, the bridges, the rivers they used to cross. The places he and his family and friends used to play. He hadn't been there since he was twelve, yet these memories came flooding back.

As we made our way along the winding paths, we would pass little old ladies with scarves tied around their heads, their faces deeply wrinkled from years in the sun and their hands angularly shaped by a lifetime of working the land. They would smile and wave as we passed. Some stopped for a chat, quick bursts of Portuguese, in the particular Madeiran dialect. It seemed that a smile was necessary to speak this language, as every face I looked at while they were speaking seemed to be alight with happy dimples and smiling eyes. I couldn't understand much at all, but I could feel their warmth. It was a real culture shock for me, so far removed from anything I'd known growing up in Harare, and yet it was strangely grounding.

Tia Conceição gently explained that after Filomena (Johnny's mum) had left, the house was simply left behind in the exact state it was back then and slowly fell into disrepair. The original thatched roof had long since rotted away, and now a rusting tin roof stood in its place. As we came closer, I was taken aback by how small the houses were, so much smaller than I'd pictured in my head. But despite their size, they held a sense of history and heart that no grand building could match.

Before I saw Johnny's childhood home with my own eyes, I had embellished it in my own imagination. He'd told me when we were discovering each other's past that he lived in a 'double-story house', so in my mind it had blossomed into something out of a pastoral postcard: a big, broad wooden structure with multiple rooms, a wraparound balcony festooned with bougainvillea, and a graceful, winding staircase leading up to picture-clad walls. I was eager to see the place, because I wanted to keep that romantic vision intact, after all, I'd created my own fairytale around it.

As we wound our way up the steps, I began to make the realisation that the picture I had created in my mind of this grand 'double-story' house was probably very different to what I would find.

And yes, how very different it was!

We pushed open the ancient wooden door of a very ramshackle stone building. Large stones balanced expertly upon the row of stones beneath. Each carefully selected for size and shape and placed strategically, in order for them not to come tumbling down. It felt as though time had frozen the day the family left.

This old door opened into Johnny's parents' room. The thatch was long gone, replaced by the tin roof which had started to rust away. Vines were growing everywhere around the house, untethered and overgrown, branching through another few sections of broken stone walls just visible through the undergrowth. In their day, the vines would have been tended to, by his parents and any of the kids old enough to do the job.

These sections of broken stone walls were the remains of a building that was part of the house where Johnny and his siblings stayed. Not much was left of it now. We needed to use a sickle we had brought with us to cut through the thick bramble, twisted weeds and old, gnarled tree branches, which hindered our way on the path up to the property.

Inside Johnnys's parents' room, a solitary wooden kist sat beneath a simple crucifix. The wooden floorboards were worn, and a few other broken pieces of furniture were still in place. A rocking chair and a table. We carefully opened the heavy lid of the kist. Unbelievably, there lay a few sepia-toned photographs of Johnny as a boy, alongside a few letters he had penned to his mother from when he was at the orphanage. For a moment, I felt as though I was touching his soul.

The two little images, which we kept, showed Johnny, not smiling, simply sitting in a chair. One taken from the front and the other taken from the side. They're the only images we have of him from his childhood in Machico. It's hard to believe how easily our own boys could be the child in those photos. There could never be any doubt that it's Johnny in those solemn, black and white pictures, which were most probably photos required for some type of documents. He's aged remarkably well.

We also brought the crucifix home. It was slightly damaged and tarnished from the years of sitting there with only spiders, rats and bugs to adore it. I lovingly restored it to its former glory, and it now sits in our family room in pride of place on the little home altar where we say our family Rosary and prayers each night.

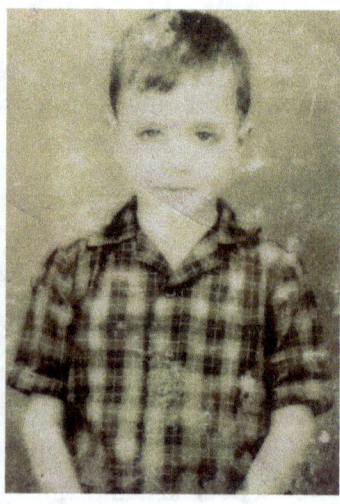

We went back out and round the side to another wooden door underneath. This room was where 'Avo' stayed – Johnny's grandmother on his dad's side. The room was now stacked with wood and building supplies for whenever, if ever, the house might be repaired.

It was an incredible feeling – placing myself into that space and trying to imagine how different his life was back then. It was completely foreign to everything I had grown up with, my own modern, westernised culture, far-flung from these stone walls. I wondered what their conversations would have been about, what clothes they might have worn and the meals that would have been prepared.

I imagined how Johnny must have clung to the promise that God would not abandon him, even though he'd lost his family and lived his teenage years away from his birthplace and familiar childhood surroundings. That's when I made the realisation that every moment of that simple life, and the hardships following on after, had been stepping stones, carrying him from the foot of that Madeiran mountain, all the way to me.

As the days passed, many more pieces of the family puzzle came to light. Stories that had been hidden or whispered about Johnny, since he had left for Rhodesia to join his father and who was, for all they knew, lost or presumed dead.

During this honeymoon visit I spent many afternoons sitting with Avo, (Johnny's grandmother on his mother's side) while she hand-sewed beautiful pieces of fabric to be used as tray cloths, tablecloths and little furniture coverings. She was dressed in black, still mourning the death of her husband, who had died many years before. She was always with a rosary at hand when she wandered down below to the church for daily Mass and prayers. She was a deeply devout woman, who didn't speak much, but I felt a connection to her.

I kept thinking how, after all those years apart, it must have been almost impossible for her to truly comprehend what was happening. Joao Luis, her grandson, the boy she'd long believed to be gone forever, was now standing there before her, alive and well. What must that have felt like? To hug him and hear his voice, after carrying the weight of loss for so long. I also wondered about the many years in between, and how difficult the situation must have been for her, navigating the heartbreak and complicated families of her daughters. I suppose the quiet ache of uncertainty was offered up in prayer.

Clearly, there had been a rift in the family, and it seemed to run deep. The Venezuelan branch of the family had since lost almost all ties with the Madeiran side. And the African side, living a completely separate life across the ocean, was only loosely linked. José Senior's contentious marriage to the other sister, and his annual trips back to Madeira, were probably widening the gap more than bridging it. The family was splintered, scattered across continents, each faction carrying its own version of the story.

Everyone still spoke respectfully of Johnny's father, but underneath it all, I sensed a quiet relief that he no longer lived permanently on the island. His annual visits with his wife, Tia Katarina, and their daughter Anna, weren't easy for anyone in the family. The bond between the two sisters, Tia Conceição and Tia Katarina, still seemed strong, and I suppose it had been forged through understanding, pain and loyalty.

Clearly Tia Conceição had come to accept Tia Katarina's decision to marry the man who had once been married to their other sister, Filomena – Johnny's mother. It was a tangled, deeply complicated family dynamic. So many rumours, so much history and so much left unspoken, but it was what it was. I did not understand it then, and to be honest, I probably never will.

We asked everyone whether they knew where Johnny's mother was living, or how we might find his siblings, but no one we spoke to seemed to have any real answers. It would be another ten years before we finally got some contact details, though that's a story for a further chapter.

Over the few weeks we spent in Madeira, Johnny's Portuguese started coming back to him, a few more words each day. It was lovely to hear, and even I started understanding a little, but only when he spoke. He spoke so slowly and carefully in short sentences, which made it easier for me to follow. Nearly every sentence was interspersed with: 'Como se diz isto?' 'How can I say?' And that little phrase is one that he frequently says to this day – only in English now: 'How can I put it to you?'

In Portuguese homes, the kitchen truly is the heart of everything. It's where the love happens, especially when there are guests around. Meals aren't just made, they're an all-day preparation with love and pride, and as a guest, you're expected to show your appreciation by eating everything served up in front of you. This, honestly, became quite a challenge. I didn't want to offend anyone by leaving food on the plate, but I didn't have a big appetite and the portions were massive. The food was absolutely delicious, rich, hearty and full of flavour – but very different to what I was used to. I had to challenge myself to get through every lovingly prepared mouthful. Sometimes I simply couldn't finish it all.

About two weeks into our visit, the queasiness started, usually at mealtimes and especially in the mornings. I'd have to excuse myself from the table, crying and in a fluster, my head spinning and my stomach churning. It was not only from the nausea, but probably also from the sheer overwhelming reality of it all. Johnny's family couldn't understand why I barely touched the huge servings of food they'd so lovingly prepared, and I just didn't have the words or the courage, to explain that it wasn't due to their cooking. It really was delicious food, but my appetite had shrunk, and I felt swallowed up by the pressure to eat it all, with a smile.

I assumed at the time it was the change in diet and larger portions, but with our daughter Renée arriving exactly nine months later, it turns out it wasn't the food at all, it was morning sickness. I think the family might have suspected this, because the mealtimes became less stressful after a few table dashes, and I noticed the older women talking amongst themselves, whilst trying not to make it obvious they were talking about me.

I'll never forget those drives around the island with Johnny's aunts, uncles and all the cousins. It felt like a wonderful dream, exploring some of the most amazing and beautiful spots in the world. Sometimes we'd be up high in the mountains, where the road literally disappeared into the clouds and then reappeared above them.

It was as if we were the only beings that existed, as everything was now hidden below the clouds. It seemed 'otherworldly.'

After winding back down from the mountaintop, the next moment we'd find ourselves hugging the edge of a steep cliff with nothing between us and the sheer drop to the depths below but a low stone wall. Driving those roads, all on the 'wrong' side, took considerable focus and skill.

Every so often, we'd pull off at tiny roadside 'miradouros', those lookout points placed in strategic locations where you could stop to take it all in and grab a quick photo. Suddenly there'd be a view so vast and green and endless, it made you want to get out and walk rather than drive. I simply couldn't drink it all in.

It was magnificent, and every bend and turn produced something even more spectacular. The villages nestled below looked as though they belonged in a storybook, and the terraced hillsides, dotted with banana trees, stretched all the way to the glittering sea.

Some days we packed a picnic and ate outdoors, pulling apart crusty *bolo do caco,* that heavenly Madeiran sweet potato bread, still warm from the village ovens. *Bolo do caco* was everywhere, nearly every home had an earth oven with sweet-potato dough baking. Avo, had loaves freshly baked when we first arrived. We'd pick wild bay leaves or fennel from the trees and scatter them on the meat we brought to cook on the open fire. Then, we washed our hands in the icy streams trickling down the rocks, water unbelievably cold and crystal clear.

MOUNTAINS OF LOVE

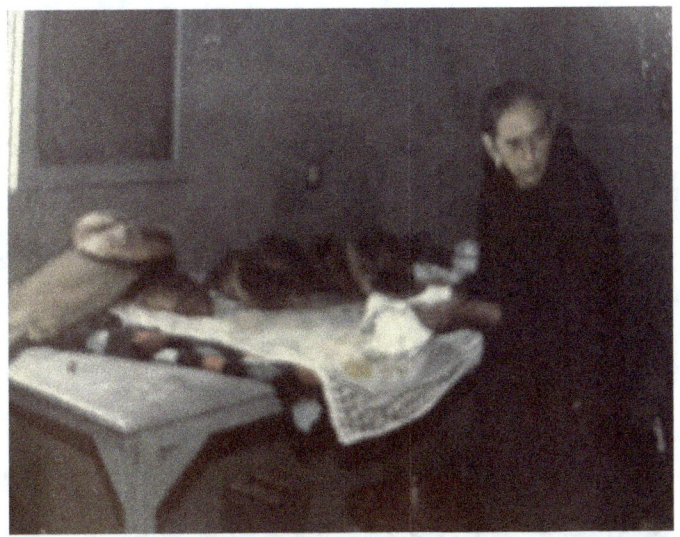

Other times, we'd stop at little restaurants clinging to the roadside – nothing fancy, just family-run places with checked tablecloths and grilled fish sizzling on metal plates. There was always the scent of garlic, olive oil, and woodsmoke in the air, and the clatter of cutlery mingled with conversation in fast, melodic Madeiran Portuguese. And of course, coffee and *Pasteis de nata* (Portuguese custard tarts) to follow after the meal.

The tunnels were extraordinary, some old and narrow, still damp from mountain mist, carved straight through the rock. We had to put the car headlights on, and they bounced off wet stone as we drove over the cobbled roads through them. As we popped out into daylight again, it was often right next to some mesmerising waterfall cascading down the cliffs. I gasped at every sight. Unless you have been to Madeira and experienced it, you can't possibly imagine the beauty and magnificence.

Then Santana, with its quaint triangular houses, white walls with red doors and windows, all trimmed with blue. Thatched roofs sloped all the way to the ground. The red geraniums, the old women in aprons, the wood smoke curling up into the sky.

Everything about Madeira was and still is utterly breathtaking. To think I was married to a man who came from this island of wild beauty, and yet, once upon a time, I hadn't even known it existed. It still astonishes me at how blessed I was to have had love lead me to a place like this, through Johnny.

We eventually returned home to the farm, Govete Ranch, where I was now not only a farmer's wife, but a mother-to-be. I'd come back with a whole new understanding of Johnny. Seeing the beautiful island he came from, hearing his story through the people who had known him as a boy, all this had added another layer to who he was. My admiration for him only grew. To most, he was merely Johnny, the successful farmer; but to me, he was so much more.

11

Corrections

Renée, our first child, was born in 1988, and then in quick succession three boys followed: Daniel, Paul and André. By the time the first two boys were born, we had already moved from Govete Ranch to manage Section F on Forrester Estates.

The Von Pezhold family had bought Forrester Estates in 1988, the year we moved to live and work there. The estate comprised of 10 sections, each named with a letter of the alphabet: A, B, C, D, E, F, H, J, I, L. Managers were employed to run the individual sections like a farm within a farm. They were responsible for crops, cattle and day-to-day operations. Certain sections were fine-tuned for specific crops, of which tobacco was a major one, and others for cattle breeding, making the whole enterprise well-integrated and highly successful. Forrester has become known as 'The Home of the Zimbabwe Boran' for its pioneering work in that breed. We were present when the artificial insemination period of the herd began in our section. It was fascinating to have witnessed this.

We took over from Hans and Shirley Maartens, who had worked with Johnny as an assistant years before, whilst he was still a bachelor. He had become part of their family, and they had very generously given him a 21st birthday celebration.

Johnny often tells stories of his farming days when he was an assistant on F Section. The stories normally surface when the kids or someone complains about how hard life is, or they don't appreciate or want to eat the food that has been made for them.

Tobacco planting season is when the important job of establishing the crop in the ground takes place and thousands of seedlings are taken from the seed beds, each individually hand planted into the neatly ridged soil of the prepared lands. Come rain or shine, it must be done at the crucial time. Planting generally coincided with the rainy season and Johnny likes to tell us how his cook would ride the motorbike five kilometres out into the land with a bowl of *Sadza* (maize-meal) porridge for him to have as breakfast. He'd take off the tea towel covering it, and while seated on an anthill, would try to wolf down the quick meal, with the rain pouring down into his bowl. It was always a rush to eat before the porridge became a very watery 'slop'.

In order for Johnny to land the sought-after job as a manager on Forrester Estates, he needed to write a letter to the General Manager and explain his intentions, as well as the reasons why he should be given the job. For most people, that might seem a simple enough task, but for Johnny, who didn't have more than a few years of formal education and a definite leaning on the dyslexic side, this letter was a big and daunting challenge.

The basic things that most people take for granted, can for others be an almost insurmountable task. He told me what he wanted to write, and I wrote it out for him to copy. My heart was breaking for him as I saw him writing, then crossing out, then taking new sheet after new sheet, only to begin again. With perseverance and determination, he got it done without any mistakes – and he, of course, landed the job.

I'm sure his farming skills and past successes through discipline and attention to detail, would have been sufficient for this job to have been awarded to him, but it was a lesson to me, to never take for granted my education and the privilege of being able to express myself on paper.

That moment was humbling and full of pride. It's one I'll never forget. Those who know Johnny might say upon first meeting him that he comes across as stubborn and almost cocky. But I like to say it's a determination and a great resilience against adversities, and a fair share of adversity and setbacks he has surely faced.

After Daniel was born, and we'd done the rounds at the local ID and registration office to get his birth registered, I started to feel that little niggling anxiety again about Johnny's passport. Every time I filled in a form with the parents' section requiring all the usual name and birthplace details, I found myself hesitating, not wanting to write down what his passport said: 'Liverpool'. It just didn't sit right anymore. The story was wearing thin. I felt it was time to sort it out properly and do things the correct way.

Well, that turned out to be a bit of a disaster.

I asked around and spoke to a few friends who'd worked in the ID department, and eventually I was pointed in the direction of someone in the Ministry of Home Affairs who might be able to help. So off Johnny went, passport in hand, to meet the official and see about having his place of birth amended.

That's when the questions started. I had not anticipated this at all. I got quite annoyed with myself that I had thought this correction was a good idea.

'Why does your passport say this?'

'Where's your birth certificate?'

'Why's it written in this weird language?'

'And where's your stooper?' (the local slang for an ID card).

As I mentioned earlier, Johnny didn't have a stooper. All he had was this passport, which had been dodgy for years. There was no official entry on record of his having arrived in Zimbabwe, and certainly nothing under the name that matched his passport. The official grew increasingly agitated and eventually slammed his fist on the desk and declared,

'You're an illegal alien!'

Just like that, his passport was cancelled. Boom. Gone. One minute he was Johnny from 'Liverpool' and the next he was a man with no country of birth.

One small consolation, though – they did at least allow him to apply for a stooper. That meant, in time, he'd be able to officially apply for a Zimbabwean passport, this time with the correct details... thank goodness. It felt like a small victory in the middle of a most unsettling day.

The next stop after that unexpected turn of events was the Portuguese embassy. We figured we may as well cover all our bases. Johnny applied for and then received a Portuguese passport. Eventually, after all the drama, he ended up with two identities again... legally! Whilst we were there at the consulate, we also registered the births of both Renée and Daniel. As fate would have it, history repeated itself, and years later down the track, Daniel found himself facing the same Portuguese name spelling issues that Johnny once had. Officially, the English version of the surname simply is not recognised on any formal documentation.

It was almost laughable that after all those years of chasing papers, correcting names and proving who he was, Johnny now was officially a dual citizen. His life was never straightforward, sometimes rather complicated, but he always managed to come out the other side standing tall.

Surviving against the odds, and defying death has been a recurring theme that runs through Johnny's life, rather like a cat with nine lives! From those terrifying close calls in the army that could have easily gone the other way, to the near-fatal train accident and later, even on Forrester's F section. Once as an assistant, and then again as a manager, after we were married.

One particular brush with death, years before I met him, whilst he was an Assistant sends a chill down my spine. Johnny had taken ill and was not able to go to work. Hans and Shirley were away on leave. Johnny had been bedridden for days, which was very out of character for him. It must have been really bad for him to not go to work. The cook reported to the manager that his boss was 'very, very sick.'

Hans and Shirley were called, and they returned from their holiday with haste. Shirley ended up changing his drenched sheets every couple of hours as he was perspiring so profusely. He had deteriorated rapidly and was delirious. They suspected it was malaria. A decision was made for Hans to rush Johnny to the hospital in Harare. They phoned ahead and arranged for the doctor to expect their arrival. Hans had recently purchased a Ford Grenada, and he drove his new car, at record speed. Hans sped that one hundred kilometres distance, reaching Andréw Fleming hospital in half the usual time.

Johnny was wheeled in and apparently the doctor at the entrance, waiting for his arrival, didn't look hopeful as to whether he'd survive. Dr French shook his head and said to Hans 'I don't think he's going to make it' – at which point Johnny sat bolt upright and in a brief lucid moment said, 'Thanks Doctor' and fell back down unconscious on the bed. Treatment began immediately, and the diagnosis was confirmed that he had cerebral malaria and was extremely lucky to have survived to tell the tale. God had more plans for him.

In 1990, Johnny had another narrow escape. His great friend Koos Steyn (God rest his soul), also managing a section on Forrester Estates, rushed Johnny through to the doctor. One evening, he had been unwell with a headache and fever. Even though we were living in Mvurwi, for some reason we saw the doctor in Mtoroshanga. We'd been to the clinic to see the doctor there, twice already, during the previous week. Initially, Johnny had been treated for a virus of some sort. He was a few days into the treatment and wasn't showing much, if any, improvement. We returned and some blood tests were done. On the second visit, the results showed it was malaria. We went back home with Johnny, who was not well at all, and started the malaria medication immediately. This treatment didn't seem to help much either. He grew progressively worse, and I realised it was serious. I was heavily pregnant and had just put the kids to sleep, and not knowing what else to do, I called Koos in the middle of the night, desperate and scared.

I explained to him that our GP's partner, Dr Chitepo, whom I'd fortunately managed to track down on an after-hours number, (remember this was not in the days of smart phones and internet), would meet him at the hospital.

Koos, without hesitation, rushed over from I section to collect Johnny. Koos was a big, strong man, and he scooped Johnny up like a baby. This giant man was holding my husband as though he were weightless. He strapped him into his car and drove like crazy straight to the hospital. Koos was very sceptical that the doctor would be there, but sure enough, he was ready and waiting when Koos arrived carrying Johnny in his arms again from the car. It was cerebral malaria – again. But by some miracle, and with the right treatment, Johnny pulled through and bounced back to full health. Koos quite possibly saved his life that night.

How many lives does one man get?

Koos and Johnny used to play rugby in Mvurwi in their bachelor days. This was before Koos had moved to I section. They stayed together in the assistant's house on F section. After rugby matches and training, they would spend many, merry hours at the club and then drive home afterwards, certainly not in a sober state. Guardian angels would have been on double duty for sure.

Late one night, returning from the club, Johnny was behind the wheel in his BMW Cheetah, his pride and joy, with Koos as a passenger. Then, out of nowhere, a large animal, probably a wild pig, appeared on the tarmac. Koos shouted out, 'Careful Johnny, don't hit that thing!' It was too late.

There was a thud and a screech, and the car came to a grinding halt. Koos burst out laughing between the shock and absurdity of what just happened, and then commented through laughs, 'Ja man, now look at your bonnet!'

They climbed out and surveyed the scene. Johnny made his classic move when shocked and rubbed his head with his hands. The bonnet and front of his BMW were completely crumpled, and the creature was nowhere to be seen. It must have disappeared into the bush.

The front end was damaged enough that driving it further was out of the question. As for the two of them, well, let's just say they were probably in no condition to be behind the wheel in the first place. They decided to walk home and check back in the morning. I can only imagine the conversation between the two of them, drunkenly discussing how big the thing they hit was, and laughing at what had just transpired.

At first light and in a slightly more sober state, Johnny decided he should wake Koos up so they could go pick up the car. Johnny, ever resourceful, came up with a brilliant idea that they should search for the animal. Maybe they could sell it and make some money to repair the damage to the car.

They dashed off to the crash site. Of course there was no sign of anything, what were they thinking? It had taken off and was long gone. Its big body had made light work of the car and escaped into the bush. The reality was – no pig or whatever they hit, and a scrunched-up BMW that could not be driven!

Koos, the gentle giant, was on his haunches without hesitation, and used his mighty, brute strength. He heaved the front of the car back out into place, just enough so that it could be driven again. Those two guys were full of nonsense when they were together. I would love to have been a fly on the wall to witness even half of the mischief they got up to.

12

Eles' Gate Crash

It was a Sunday, and I had returned from Johannesburg, South Africa, the day before. My brother John was getting married, and I'd driven with all the kids, four of them at the time, to be at the wedding. Little André was only about nine months old. Renée was going to be a flower girl, and I was going to arrange the flowers and make the bouquets and button-holes.

Johnny had needed to stay on the farm, so my friend Kathy and her two kids, plus a friend's maid (my maid didn't have a passport), made the trip down to South Africa in our VW Kombi. Kathy and her kids went on to Durban. It was a fun and interesting trip; we two mums, a maid and six kids. We had a lovely few weeks preparing for and then celebrating my brother's marriage. On Saturday after the wedding, my brother John had hitched a ride with me and the kids back home to the farm. It was great to have had a hand with the twelve-hour drive, especially as I would have had to stop each time I needed to feed André, had I been on my own. John needed to be in Harare for some business and had planned to fly back to Johannesburg that next day, Sunday.

Since I had the chance, I decided to go to Mass before dropping John at the airport. Tidy, our gardener, came along as he often did when I went into town. This was partly to keep an eye on the car and partly to help with the kids. The other older kids stayed home with Johnny and only André came with me, as I was still breastfeeding him. He rode in the back of the bakkie, snug in a little cot inside the fibreglass canopy. We'd put in a mattress and cushions to make it comfy for the kids whenever we went on our road trips.

Mass finished and I dropped John at the airport, then set off home to the farm. I'd just reached the climb past Msonedi, and I suddenly realised I was drifting towards the steep embankment. I had briefly fallen asleep. When I 'woke up', my brain hadn't quite caught up to my heart. In my shock, I yanked the wheel too hard to the right, and consequently I lost control. The bakkie rolled.

I remember everything clearly, in slow motion. The crunch of metal, the screech of tyres and glass shattering. The canopy burst apart. Tidy was flung out and landed in the bush. André was thrown out of his pram and had rolled along the road. The truck rolled once, then landed on its side after a half revolution. If it had continued to roll onto the roof, André would not have survived.

I 'came to' hanging upside down, still strapped into my seatbelt, probably the one thing that had saved my life.

The cab roof had caved into a vee shape, with sharp metal frighteningly close to my head. I remember looking around and thinking, how do I get out? And then the sickening thought hit me: André! Tidy!

I scrambled out through the gaping hole where the windscreen had once been and saw André lying on the tar, the back of his head swollen, and his little fists black with stuck-on tar.

Tidy was sitting by the roadside, dazed, his face swollen and bleeding. The truck was a mangled mess in the middle of the road... and I was screaming and crying. I rushed over and scooped up André, willing him to be alive. And then, a miracle. He began to cry.

Just then, a vehicle pulled up. Two men jumped out and thoughtfully switched off my still-running engine, and then offered to take us to the hospital. One of the men stayed behind to warn traffic, stopping anyone from ploughing into the wreck I had just caused. Tidy climbed in with us, looking battered but assuring me he was OK.

Being a Sunday, there was no doctor on duty at Mvurwi Hospital. I asked the kind man to take us to Malvern House, where I could call Johnny and arrange for a doctor. There were no mobile phones back then, so the drive felt like an eternity. I cradled André closely, trying to feed him to keep him calm.

When the matron at Malvern House phoned Johnny, he was with Koos. She told him, 'Your wife's had an accident; she's fine, but the baby's not.' Johnny was in the car before the words had left her mouth. Koos went along with him, as Johnny feared the worst. But he later told me that the moment he arrived and heard André crying, he knew he would be alright.

The doctor met us at the hospital. My neck ached, I had a few cuts and bruises, and Tidy's face was a mess. André had a lump the size of a tennis ball on the back of his head and grazes on his little hands and feet. Instinctively, he had put his hands up to cover his face as he rolled along the tar, softened from the midday sun. Miraculously, that was the extent of the injuries.

The doctor ordered X-rays just to be sure. We had to wait half an hour for the very old machine to warm up, but when the results came back, no major injuries were apparent. Quite incredible.

While we were being checked over, Johnny and Koos went to fetch the bakkie. The kind men who had stopped were still there, guarding my handbag and other things. Between them, Johnny and Koos flipped the vehicle upright, and big, strong Koos managed to pull out the bent panels, and they towed it home.

When I got back, seeing the wreck was sobering. *How had we walked away from that?* The truth is, that long trip to South Africa with the kids, the wedding chaos, then the immediate turn-around drive back to Harare had all been too much. I hadn't realised just how exhausted I was until it had nearly cost us our lives.

After that day, I was a terrible passenger. My hands would grip the seat at the slightest jolt. It took years before I could sit in a car without bracing for the crash I was sure was coming.

Let me tell you more about our time as managers on F Section, where our family had now grown to four kids in as many years; Renée, and then the three boys, Daniel, Paul and André. We had many fun times in the years we were there. A massive, beautiful garden, with a tennis court and rose garden. It really was glorious and a wonderful place for the kids to grow up. We had made a great, big tree house for them to play in. They loved it, as did all the children that came over to play.

At some point in 1991, a herd of elephants had been chased across the Great Dyke Mountain Range and had found themselves on Forrester Estates, wandering between a few of the sections. They were becoming quite a nuisance in the area, terrifying the workers, as well as damaging crops and stomping on irrigation pipes and fencing.

It was incredibly beautiful watching these massive beasts up close but knowing they had been chased out of their usual habitat. A plan needed to be made to try to shift them back where they belonged, in their natural environment.

One Friday afternoon, we were driving between the sections. We were heading east on our farm, and the neighbour's wife was heading west. Just as we approached the gate, a few elephants suddenly appeared over the hill. Both vehicles stopped to watch in awe as these beautiful animals walked in our direction, on their way across the road between our two cars. The elephants decided they quite liked the spot right there in the middle of the dirt road. They were unfazed by our presence as we sat quietly watching the giant beasts.

You never quite realise the size of an elephant until you are close to them. We were delighted that we could witness this moment. It was magnificent. However, the neighbour's wife was in rather a hurry as she needed to fetch the kids from the school pickup point and couldn't wait and 'elephant watch' any longer. In those days, we always travelled with a worker, for safety and to help with gate-opening and such. So, she quickly instructed the worker to go 'shoo the elephants away!' I'm guessing she thought you could 'shoo' elephants just like you would 'shoo' flies away!

The elephants did not want to be 'shooed' away and began to flap their big ears, starting to mock charge at the poor worker. He'd been given his instruction, and wanted to obey, so he took off his hat and waved at the elephants, trying to move them off the road. He climbed onto the fence post, which didn't even increase his height to half that of the biggest elephant.

ELES' GATE CRASH

The worker tried to signal to Evelyn that she should reverse, as now the elephants were showing signs of frustration and had started to trumpet and throw their long trunks towards him. He was frantically signing to his Madam to *go back, go back*. What made Evelyn think he was signing *come through, come through,* I have no idea, but in a flash, she was racing forward in the truck. That angered the elephants even more, and now we had a rather desperate situation. The worker on the fence post, angry elephants trumpeting and looking as though they would charge any second... and Evelyn about to drive into the chaos!

We were all extremely worried. In a desperate panic, the worker had darted back to the car and jumped in with haste. He was banging the side of the vehicle in an attempt to frighten the elephants away, and Evelyn now had her foot flat, speedily reversing back down the road. We just waited patiently, albeit very nervously, and the big grey beasts eventually went on their merry way.

Looking back, we can laugh at that crazy situation, but it could have all ended very differently.

F Section featured one of the best clay tennis courts in the district. March, the gardener, was an expert at watering and rolling it and consequently after his hours, sometimes days, of preparation, we were able to host many a tennis party, or practise sessions and coaching from home.

It was also one of the 'outside' courts used during the annual Mvurwi tennis festival; the very tennis tournaments that had featured in our meeting and dating. We'd come full circle.

It was a blessing to have had the opportunity to live and work on such a beautiful estate with stunning views in every direction. I would often just stare out of the big windows of the farmhouse and be in absolute wonderment at the rolling hills, the blue-coloured dyke in the background and vibrant colours of the Msasa trees, every autumn shade imaginable; deep reds, browns, yellows, oranges and varying hues of green. It was simply breathtaking. I really do long for those unbelievably magnificent Zimbabwe landscapes. Truly, my heart still beats to the African rhythm.

13

On Our Own

In early 1992, we spent many hours of working out budgets and visiting half a dozen banks in order to try and secure a loan, as we wanted to purchase a farm of our own. We were successful in getting approval and finally found our dream farm in the adjacent district of Horseshoe.

We went first to look at the farm, and I can distinctly remember driving in and thinking *this place is completely out of our league*. I believed we could never afford an amazing place like that – a big double-story house with an attic, set in one of the most beautifully landscaped gardens I'd seen. Johnny and I both had the 'if it's meant to be, it'll be' attitude, but we hoped and prayed … that it would be!

Somehow, God looked with favour on us and answered our prayers, and we were able to make Tiaseka Farm (tee-AH-seh-kuh) our home for nearly the next ten years, until we were finally forced to say goodbye.

The garden was my absolute pride and joy, a real slice of paradise. From the balcony off our bedroom, we could look out over the whole expanse of the garden. A little canal traced its way around the edges of the big granite rocks, and from the highest rock, a waterfall tumbled down, threading through orchids and ferns which nestled in every crevice. Tall, dramatic Spathodea trees would burst into fiery red and orange blooms, creating a canopy of colour.

To add to the magic (or chaos), great big troops of monkeys would sometimes decide our garden was the best place for a playground and turf war. Some afternoons they would descend down the kopje (cop-ee) and swing through the Spathodea branches, screeching and chattering. It was immense fun to watch them from the safety of the bedroom balcony.

Off to one side, on the upper level of the garden, was the swimming pool. It was cleverly designed and had been built into the rock face. The kids spent endless summer days leaping off the rock into the deep end, squealing with delight. Echoes of 'Marco Polo' rang out just as they had done when I was a child playing with my buddies in my best friend's family pool.

Many days whilst out in the garden, the younger kids would beg Tidy to take them for rides around the place in the wheelbarrow. It was a great treat for them to be perched in the barrow, as if they were some kind of mini royals being paraded about. They squealed with delight as soon as they spotted the gardener out with the barrow and scrambled to jump aboard, never wanting the rides to end.

Right beside the pool was another piece of garden where we had a tiny chapel. I designed a stained-glass window for it: an image of *Our Lady of Perpetual Succour*, a special devotion of ours, especially because her feast day is the 27th of June – our wedding anniversary. That window has followed us halfway around the world and is now here in Perth, just waiting for us to complete building a grotto, not only to hold the window, but also to properly house some large statues I have recently sculpted.

The chapel was a peaceful haven. We had Mass said there, usually once a month or at least every couple of months. The parish priest would drive out for a weekend break and say Mass for our family and friends in the area. It gave the place a sense of calm and grace, something we all needed with the general madness of life.

As if that garden wasn't big enough, I went and cleared another few sections. Past the canal, next to the waterfall rock, we created another native garden with a little dam. Gums from the farm were made into a couple of wooden bridges and a deck that led to the perfect spot, just calling for a tennis court. So, we went ahead and made one! A proper clay court that could rival the one at Forrester's F Section. We even installed floodlights so we could play during the evening.

March, our other gardener and our 'court specialist' had followed us from Forrester Estates to Tiaseka, so we knew we would have the expert to maintain it. The view from there stretched across to the lands near the dam, which Johnny had recently built. It was absolutely breathtaking. Behind the house, another large kopje was perfect for the kids to clamber up to the top and explore. It became our front-row seat for the solar eclipse in November 1994.

A group of friends came out to the farm, and together we climbed to the top of the kopje, settling on the flattest spot for a picnic lunch. Then, for the most extraordinary and almost surreal few minutes, the sun slipped behind the moon and the sky turned dark.

The world seemed to hold its breath in the stillness. It felt very strange as we all slipped on our special viewing glasses to witness this historical moment. Then, about half an hour later, it was 'day' again. The birds began to chirp as though it were sunrise. It was an unforgettable day.

Johnny had stocked the dam with both bass and bream fish. We would go down some afternoons or early evenings, with fishing rods and flying ants for bait, to see if we could catch any. The kids loved fishing, and on occasion we would take the little boat, loaded with a picnic, and we would ride around on the dam. Thankfully, this dam didn't have a resident crocodile, unlike the big dam on

Forrester F Section. Apparently, that croc had sneakily taken the odd calf drinking at the water's edge.

Tiaseka Farm was always full of surprises. Sometimes when we drove down to the lands to check on the crops, we'd be rewarded with the most magnificent sight of a herd of kudu grazing quietly at the edge of the fields. We would usually first spot their incredible spiral horns, and they'd lift their regal heads to watch us with calm, curious eyes. We'd sit in the truck in complete silence, hardly daring to breathe, soaking in the beauty of it all. Whenever we encountered them, that feeling of awe never became old. Even though poaching was becoming an increasing problem around that time, the kudu, somehow, always seemed to return to our bottom lands, as if they knew they were safe there. Alongside them, smaller buck like duikers and bushbuck would dart through the long grass, their quick movements catching the light. Each sighting was a special treat and a reminder of how wild and wonderful Tiaseka was.

When we were first married and living on Govete Ranch, Johnny rescued a baby duiker, as its mother had been killed. He named it *Dykey* and lovingly bottle-fed it until it was strong enough to fend for itself. It was the cutest little thing, with soft, dark eyes and enormous eyelashes. It had the sweetest nature. Johnny built a little enclosure for it in the garden, though that didn't stop it from sneaking into my flower beds and nibbling on the roses whenever it could. *Dykey* adored Johnny and would come trotting over for a scratch behind the ears whenever he was near. Sadly, while we were away on holiday, we came home to the heartbreaking news that *Dykey* had died. Rumour had it that one of the labourers had taken a liking to the idea of 'duiker stew'. I was absolutely shattered. It's funny how those little creatures find their way into your heart.

Of course, it wasn't only the gentle, furry kind of wildlife we encountered. Snakes were a regular feature of farm life – mostly harmless if left alone, but enough to keep me on edge.

One day, the crop guard came running to tell us there was a massive *'nyoka'* (snake) in the trees. Naturally, we had to see for ourselves, so off we went in the truck, not far from the house, I might add, until we reached a gathering of half the labour force staring up in awe. Draped between two trees was the biggest python I had ever seen. Its body shimmered with its exquisitely patterned scales, coiled like a rope between the branches. One end in the left tree, the other looping around the right, its tail dangling almost to the ground. I swear it must have been at least five metres long! You could see the trail in the dust where it had slithered across the road. I kept a very respectful distance as I don't consider snakes to be my friends. I did manage to get a photo from the safety of the truck before it disappeared back into the bush. Judging by its size, it was well-fed on Tiaseka's resident wildlife!

Then there were the wild pigs. Mischievous and destructive, they loved to dig up the lands and root through the crops. A few of the adults had been shot for causing havoc, and Johnny rescued two of the babies. These tiny, squealing bundles of trouble were brought in for bottle-feeding, of course (because that's just Johnny), and they soon grew to become our much-loved farm pets, Potjie (poy-kee, meaning 'little pot' in Afrikaans) and Streaky. They'd wander around the garden near the gate, snorting happily, following Johnny like little dogs, and entertaining the kids for hours. They were great characters. Farm life was never dull.

Johnny's absolute passion was, and still is, birds, the feathered variety, of course. What started as a few budgie aviaries turned into a full-blown bird sanctuary. Eventually, he had around 400 aviaries, filled with birds from all over the globe. Parakeets, Lorikeets, Goffin Cockatoos, Eclectus parrots, peacocks, pheasants and even a pair of Macaw parrots. It was his daily ritual to walk around the aviaries, mug of tea in hand, talking to his feathered friends. Often there was screeching and a general cacophony of noise emanating from that area of the garden.

Early on, soon after moving to Tiaseka, we had built a schoolroom, as we had decided to teach our kids from home. I did the teaching for the first year and then we employed a lovely teacher who lived on the farm in the cottage. It was a very special few years, having the kids at home to do their learning. The kids eventually went to school in about grade 3 and that meant the room became available to be the 'bird' room.

There were incubators, medications and all kinds of equipment for the birds in that room. Johnny used to feed the little birds as they hatched, their feeding routine not too dissimilar to our human infants! Just as I would be getting up to breastfeed one of the kids, he'd usually be going over to the bird nursery to feed his baby birds. Johnny had trained one of his workers, and he'd become the dedicated 'bird man'.

Most of the aviaries housed breeding pairs, and over the years, Johnny reared hundreds of birds of many different varieties. His pride and joy was the big round aviary where the African Greys could properly stretch their wings. Leaving them behind when we moved was heartbreaking. They were all rehomed, but I know Johnny still misses them.

14

Snapped

Along with all the tennis leagues, competitions and festivals that kept us busy, there was also the annual Mvurwi squash festival, in which Johnny, Mini and a few other mates usually played.

According to the format, matches were played in timed sessions with both courts running concurrently. The aim wasn't simply to win, but to score as many points as possible before the bell rang. At the end of the day, all the points were tallied up to declare the winning team. It was competitive and chaotic but lots of good fun. Some players raced through their matches, chalking up points as though there was no tomorrow.

One particular squash tournament, though, has stuck in my memory. The club was a hive of activity that weekend; children running around, neighbouring farmers out playing golf, bowls happening on the green, social tennis, polocrosse, and a lively crowd in the bar. I think the only sport not being played at Mvurwi Club that day was rugby.

By Sunday afternoon, the squash section was in full swing. I had noticed a commotion from that side, so I wandered over, curious to see what it was about. Lo-and-behold, there was Johnny, being helped along by two mates, one on each side, his arms slung over their shoulders as he hopped on one leg. Clearly, something had gone very wrong. Then I heard what had caused the stir.

Apparently, Johnny had been doing very well against his opponent, desperately racking up points as the clock ticked down, when suddenly there was a sound like a gunshot. The spectators swore they heard it too. But it wasn't a gun at all. No, it was Johnny's Achilles tendon snapping like a pistol crack. He went down in a heap, his leg refusing to hold him up. His opponent, blissfully unaware of the drama, kept on serving and smashing away, delighted with the stream of unreturned points until the bell eventually rang.

Johnny, confused and not yet in pain, couldn't understand why he simply couldn't stand. Then Chris Sheppard, who was on scoring duty for the match, dashed onto the court, took one look, and gasped. (Chris, by the way, is an incredibly talented photographer, and he helped with many of the photos in this book). Johnny had completely severed his Achilles tendon. Chris could actually poke his finger right into the gap at the back of Johnny's ankle. With the next players waiting, Johnny had to be carried off, which is when I saw him hopping to the change rooms.

I quickly arranged for our maid to watch the kids, loaded Johnny into the Kombi, thankfully with the back seats always laid flat (for the kids to sleep when needed) and off we went on our 'ambulance run' to hospital in Harare. He was admitted immediately and prepared for surgery the next day. The surgeon shook his head in admiration and declared that Johnny had done a 'really good job' of it, with not a single tendon fibre left intact. The repair was delicate work, strand by strand stitched back together. No small feat. (Yes... pun intended!)

That was the beginning of many months in plaster, his cast stretching from his toes up to his knee, his foot repositioned every three months to slowly stretch the tendon back into place. The kids thought it was brilliant fun, decorating Dad's cast with graffiti, while Johnny spent half of his days shoving a ruler down the side of it to scratch his itchy leg.

Farm life for Johnny in this situation was less amusing. Once Johnny had been helped upstairs in our double-storeyed-house, he had to remain there for the first few weeks. Meals on trays, endless cups of tea ferried up the stairs, and long hours spent sulking on the balcony, gazing out at the garden where the kids played. All the while, his birds chirped merrily, without him able to do his daily ritual of walking around the aviaries. He was utterly frustrated at being cooped up.

Worse still, it was tobacco curing season. Normally, Johnny would check the barns two or three times a night, adjusting temperatures, testing humidity, inspecting the leaves. Without him, I had to step up as his stand-in 'barn-boy.' For Johnny, it was like tasting food over the phone. Imagine my trying to describe the subtle colours of the leaves without him being physically able to see them hanging in the barns.

Johnny: 'Is it orange?'

Me: 'No, more of a deep reddish-yellowy brown? Or maybe yellow-orange? Actually, it might have a tinge of green.'

He also wanted me to smell the leaves, which was a task somewhat beyond my expertise. I had no clue.

Me: 'It kind of smells like toffee.'

Johnny: 'What do you mean – toffee?'

Me: 'Well I don't know, it just smells nice, like tobacco smells.'

Poor Johnny. He was going nuts.

The pressure was real. 'Keep the temperature at 45 to 50 degrees, not too hot or the barn will burn down, but not too cool or the leaves will get *sponge.*'

Eventually, Johnny couldn't stand leaving it all to me. He tackled the stairs and 'crutched' his way down, but even then, it wasn't enough. The staff finally came up with a plan, and they plonked him into a wheelbarrow with a special chair rigged on top and trundled him to the barns. Just like the kids did, only now, he was the 'big kid'. That image still makes me laugh. Salvation came a bit later in the form of a borrowed electric wheelchair. It was a contraption built from a ride-on mower engine. It was slow and rather cumbersome, but it gave Johnny back his freedom, and soon he was zipping (well, puttering) around the barns and the workshops. He could even be driven to the lands. He was himself again.

Not that the 'crutches' days were without drama. One afternoon, I heard a rustling in the cupboard next to the fireplace. Assuming it was a rat, I slid the door open, only to come face-to-face with a very angry Mozambican cobra, with its hood up ready to spit its deadly venom. I screamed wildly, as you know, I absolutely do not do snakes! Johnny was immediately summoned, on his crutches. He hobbled down the stairs and donned a pair of sunglasses for eye protection. He quickly dispatched the snake with one crutch, while balancing on the other. Typical Johnny.

It was an eventful curing season, to put it mildly. Between the dodgy 'long-distance barn checking,' the wheelbarrow rides, and the snake fights, I think we were both glad when all the tobacco was finally slat-packed and in the shed.

The tobacco sold well that year, so I can't have been too hopeless as his assistant after all.

Johnny's ankle eventually healed back to 100% and he liked to say that his wired-up tendon was much stronger than the original. Still, it had been a long, gruelling six months getting there.

In 1994, we welcomed our fifth child, sweet Monique; our first baby without my parents nearby. They'd gone to live in the UK for a couple of years, and I really missed having Mum around after Monique's birth. They had been living in South Africa and would drive up from Joburg quite often, and always when I was about to have a baby, but this time, I was flying solo. The kids loved having Bomma and Granddad to stay, and I think my parents loved coming to visit us on the farm too. By 1997, they were back living in Joburg and making their regular visits again.

The kids grew up in the beautiful outdoors. The huge front garden area usually became the golf range, and many days were spent hitting air balls across the lawn. André seemed to develop his love for golf about this time and although only just able to walk, sporting a bulky cloth nappy, he would waddle around picking up the golf balls for Granddad and then, determined not be left out, would have a swing himself with a miniature golf club that Tidy, the gardener had fashioned for him. He had a natural talent for the game, and by the age of five, some of the professional players who saw him hitting the ball, when we took him along to the country club to play alongside us, were absolutely astonished at his brilliance. That probably explains why he is a scratch handicap today.

Johnny and I both loved sport, so the kids grew up surrounded by all our home-made facilities on the farm. We had cricket nets and a wicket near the gate, so the boys could bowl to each other and then, of course, swing the bat to hit the balls as hard as they possibly could. Between tennis balls, golf balls and cricket balls, we had dozens of smashed windows in the house over the years.

When not at school, the days were filled with adventure. They built dams for hours on end, digging into the mud and pouring in countless buckets of water until, at last, their little reservoirs spilled over. They floated little boats, created with twigs and leaves, along the garden canal or their mini 'rivers', winding through from their overflowing dams. They loved playing 'Hide and Seek' on the garden kopje, darting and squealing as they clambered over the rocks, usually firing toy guns. Other times, they'd wander down to the workshops, pretending to drive like real farmers, while sitting in the seats of the tractors, and, if they were especially lucky, they'd get to ride along with the driver.

We were very blessed to have wonderful staff who were very protective of our kids. And we were blessed to have the farm itself, every corner waiting for a special use. It was an idyllic life for our family, and we'll be forever grateful that we were able to experience it.

I always found plenty of time for gardening, and with so many helpers, the big jobs never felt overly daunting. I spent many afternoons with a paintbrush in hand, or arranging a vase full of my garden flowers, or busy at my sewing machine. Back then, I used to make all my own clothes and most of the kids' outfits too. If they'd been old enough to notice or care what they were wearing, I'm not sure I would have been able to get away with it. Nowadays, when they flip through old photographs, the eyerolls and questions are usually the same: 'Mum, what on earth am I wearing? Why did you dress me like that?'

Looking back, I smile, because in those moments, I see not just the 'groovy' clothes, but the fun-filled days themselves; the sun on the lands, the daily rhythm of farm life and the joy of raising a family in a place that, for all its challenges, gave us so much.

15

Trespassing

In 1999, little Philip came along. Thank heavens for our new VW Kombi van which we had acquired, or we'd have had to drive a two-car convoy, with our expanding brood. Zimbabwe was becoming increasingly unstable by the day; safety was a real issue. We had gone back to the safety precautions of the bush war days and made iron 'burglar bars' for our windows, doors and veranda area. Many farming families were starting to make plans to leave the country.

Emigrating hadn't really been on our radar. We really did think we'd be the last ones left to turn out the lights. In truth, we had no idea where we'd go if we were unable to stay on Tiaseka. Possibly South Africa, as my parents lived there, or we could possibly go to Madeira. However, the thought of moving to a foreign country with the kids and having to learn a new language or fit into a different culture was overwhelming. It seemed to be a completely far-fetched scenario. Until it became a reality.

A number of our friends had started talking about Australia and investigating the possibility of immigrating there. But that was the other side of the world and far, far away.

Neighbouring districts were reporting some very tense situations on their farms, and it was only a matter of time before Horseshoe would be affected too. We met with an immigration agent so we could have a 'plan B', just in case the proverbial 'pawpaw hit the fan.'

We discussed our options and finally decided we should join our friends in their Australian immigration endeavours. And, just like that, the idea of leaving Tiaseka Farm became more than just a conversation over a cup of tea and everyone else's plan. Now it was ours too!

We began the application for immigration on a '127-Business' visa. Our destination was to be Perth, in the west of Australia. I had to consult the atlas, despite my A-level in geography. I needed to see where exactly we were headed. Mountains of paperwork needed to be completed, scanned and posted. All our original certificates and documents needed to be copied and certified. At the start of the application process, all of the kids had been registered on my passport, but that was due to expire.

New government rules required that each child must have their own passport. Johnny too was now eligible to apply for a passport, having waited the requisite period of time for his citizenship, following the past cancellation debacle. He had previously received his metal 'stooper'. So, we traipsed down to the passport office with all the kids in tow. It was quite a challenge getting each child to 'not smile' for the passport photo and to 'sign' their name. They all felt like 'grown-ups' making a signature. None of us had dressed in the necessary plain coloured top with a collar, so, in turn, we all donned the grey jacket that the office had available for applicants such as us. The exercise was not as easy as Johnny's original passport application in his bachelor days, and there certainly would be no 'Liverpool' given as birthplace either.

In due course, we each received our new Zimbabwean passport, and we were now ready to begin the Australian immigration paperwork. As we each needed a separate visa application filed, my job as scribe took forever to prepare all eight sets of the documentation.

I'd never even set foot in Australia, and I wasn't entirely convinced whether it was the right move. From the pictures and videos I'd seen, it looked like an impressive and beautiful place, with blue skies, wide open spaces, and a climate not too different from what we were used to. At least the people spoke English, even if it did come with that strange, 'sing-songy' twang!

Still, it all felt rather surreal. It was both exciting and completely daunting at the same time.

But I was ready. Ready to get out of the madness. The growing tensions in the country had started to feel like a heavy weight pressing down on us, and the farm was no longer the safe haven it once had been.

The government's so-called 'Land Reform' programme had thrown the country into turmoil. What was meant to be about redistributing land had instead descended into chaos and rampant violence. Across the rural areas, gangs of thugs, backed by the ruling ZANU-PF party, stormed onto farms, forcing white farmers off their land through sheer intimidation and brutality.

Friends of ours had been murdered. It was utterly horrendous. Farms were being taken, most with force, some with terrible violence, one after the other, week by week. Families were being thrown into turmoil, forced to pack up everything at a moment's notice and start over in Harare, clinging to whatever pieces they could salvage from the life they'd built. Most had no fall-back profession or job they could now do. Everyone was desperately making whatever plan they could.

It was heartbreaking and terrifying to witness. The writing was well and truly on the wall, and it was no longer safe to be on our farm. It wasn't a question of if it would happen to us, but when. And so, Australia began to feel less like an 'unknown' and more like our lifeline.

The Zimbabwe dollar was in freefall, losing value by the day, and it had become nearly impossible to obtain hard cash. The kids no longer had the freedom to ride their bikes through the lands, climb the kopje or walk down and play next to the dam in the way they once had. Those carefree days were over.

So-called 'war veterans', many barely out of their teens (and therefore too young to have fought in the bush war), began moving onto the land, wielding a new kind of power. They pegged out plots all over the farm and built shacks in the middle of the planted fields, or wherever it suited them. It didn't matter that the land was ours. According to them, it now belonged to them. That's what the government officials told them.

Our irrigation pumps and farm equipment were being stolen, and our livestock was being slaughtered. We were told that we couldn't go anywhere near the pegged areas. We were even told that we were trespassing on our own farm. It was government-backed madness, and it was frightening.

By this time, I was pregnant – again! We began to spend most weekends in town, slowly moving what we could off the farm, selling things or putting them aside for the great Aussie move, if and when, our visa was granted. Australian visas could take up to two years to process, and we were not at all certain whether we'd be successful. Of course, I would soon have to begin a ninth application, to include the new addition on the paperwork as soon as our seventh baby arrived.

Darling little Felicity arrived in mid-2001, our bright little blessing, born right in the middle of the chaos. The country's healthcare system had crumbled. There had been a brain drain, because many doctors had already fled. The hospital staff were constantly on strike, and there were no nurses available on the birth ward the day that Felicity arrived. I had delivered her by an emergency C-section, as she had turned around inside my belly, and no amount of manipulation by the gynaecologist would convince her to go head down. In addition, my blood pressure had skyrocketed, and I was showing signs of pre-eclampsia.

Despite my condition, I felt I would be better off leaving the hospital, with its skeleton staff, and going home to rest and be cared for there.

My parents had travelled up from Joburg, as they always did, to help with the new baby. Dad and Johnny had both driven to the hospital to visit me, and afterwards, they continued on to the farm to sort out business there. The idea was that Mum would drive me back to the house in Harare. But once she was behind the wheel, I could see she was overwhelmed. Not having driven in a while and not knowing the Harare roads, she froze. She didn't feel confident enough to drive. Renée also needed to be fetched from boarding school at Arundel, so, despite the emergency caesarean the day before, I decided to do the driving myself. In those days, you simply did what had to be done.

16

Hostage

Then came the day I'll never forget – it was a Friday in October 2001. I was making the usual two-hour drive to Barwick School to fetch the kids from weekly boarding school. In the afternoon, I was then going to drive a further two-and-half hours on to Karoi for an interschool swimming gala at Rydings School.

Philip was Johnny's little shadow and had stayed behind with him on the farm while I took off on the school run. There was a farm equipment auction on the neighbour's farm that day, and Johnny needed to attend it. Our lovely, trusted maid, Valeria, watched Philip while Johnny was gone. She had become like part of the family.

Suddenly, out of nowhere, I started to hear panicked chatter over the farm radio network in the car. There was unrest at a local political rally. Then … I heard our farm's name mentioned. My heart dropped. I was two hours away, with no mobile phone and no way of finding out what was happening. I was gripped by fear. I continued driving, as I couldn't turn around because the kids needed to be fetched from school. I hoped that the distraction of fetching the kids and taking them to the swimming gala might help calm my fears.

Looking back, it all seems surreal, like a scene out of someone else's life. But this was very much ours. Fridays had become infamous because that was the day when the government would publish their lists of the next farms to be seized. That Friday, it was to be our turn, but we didn't know it yet.

What had unfolded was that a political rally had been held at the village school neighbouring our farm, and, as usual, it soon became a loud, volatile and hostile situation.

The organisers were fuming that most of our farm labourers hadn't pitched up to attend the rally. And they placed the blame on Johnny. They assumed he'd instructed his workers to stay away, which simply wasn't true. The reality was that they just didn't want to attend. They much preferred to stay and work.

The incensed, axe-wielding mob weren't interested in this explanation, and decided they'd march on down, straight to our farm. Apparently, they wanted to 'teach Johnny a lesson' and drag everyone to the rally, like it or not. As they made their way up the road and over the dam along the wall, they were shouting and chanting. They arrived at the gate to our house in full voice. Our security guard held strong and refused them entry through the locked gate and into the yard. The angry crowd had surrounded the property and were very intimidating. For our staff inside the yard, it was terrifying.

Inside the house, Valeria could hear the commotion going on at the gate, so she grabbed two-year-old Philip and bolted up into the attic room to hide. She wasn't taking any chances. Philip understood Shona very well for a toddler, and from the look on Valeria's face and the tone of the shouting outside, he knew something was seriously wrong.

As Johnny had gone to the auction on the next-door farm, he was completely unaware of the incoming chaos. By the time he heard the pandemonium on the radio, just as I had, he too was beside himself. Our little boy was at home alone with the maid, while a furious mob circled the house like a scene out of the movie 'Zulu'.

I continued to receive fractured updates over the radio, and my heart was racing. I was completely powerless and desperate for news. Our farm neighbour, Wilf, immediately offered to go to our farm and see what he could do. He drove right up to the chanting crowd and tactfully managed to negotiate with them. Such a brave move!

The mob had barricaded the house. No one was allowed in, and no one was allowed out. They were demanding that everyone, including Valeria, should come with them to the rally for some 'discipline'. The few staff who were still around had no real choice. They all went, leaving little Pip, hidden away in the attic. They just prayed he would stay safe and silent.

Then, and I'll never really understand how, but Wilf managed to talk his way inside. He was calm, firm and made it clear he was there for the child. Whether the mob knew Pip was there or not, I don't know. But Wilf got in, found our little boy and took him right out of the terrifying chaos, back to safety on his farm next door.

As soon as Johnny knew it was safe to do so, he raced to Wilf's house and just hugged our little Pip like he never wanted to let him go. I travelled back that afternoon with the other kids and met them at Wilf's place. It was probably a good thing that I hadn't known what was going down whilst it was happening, because I would have struggled to drive the rest of the kids home safely.

We all cried. I think we aged ten years in one afternoon. However, our little Pip was safe. And then, just as we thought we might exhale, we received the news we had blindly hoped would never come: Tiaseka had been 'compulsorily acquired' officially through a 'Section 8' order from the Government of Zimbabwe. It explained the crazy events of the day. We were given twenty-eight days in which to leave our farm. That was it. The final blow.

That night changed us. Everything we had poured our hearts into, our land, our home, our life's work, was crumbling. The writing was on the wall in bold red letters. No piece of earth was worth the risk to our lives, our kids' lives, our peace of mind, our future. 'Plan B' wasn't just an idea anymore; it had become an urgent necessity.

That traumatic Friday will never be forgotten.

We moved into Harare and commuted back and forth from the farm to try and wrap up the farming season. Reaping, curing and baling tobacco, harvesting the remaining crops in the ground, just squeezing the last bit out of the land we loved, not knowing how much longer we'd be allowed to stay.

17

Pack It Up

Anyone who has moved house, knows the stress and the logistical difficulties involved. The missing possessions, the lost things and then the precious items, broken or damaged. Now imagine moving, not by choice, but by forced necessity, and not only a house, but an entire farm. With seven kids and a strong sentimental attachment to many of our possessions, this was a near insurmountable task.

Normally when you move, there's ample time to mull things over, to decide what you really need in your new home, what's merely clutter, and what can be thrown away or sold. Then there are the things that are kept purely because you like them (even if it's a box of buttons or a sparkly gift bag from 1982). But when the decision is forced upon you, and you're not sure exactly where you're going to end up living, every item suddenly takes on monumental importance.

We'd lived a full life in all those big houses, and over the years, we'd certainly accumulated a great deal of 'stuff.' Sometimes I wondered if I had inherited a touch of the hoarding gene. I'm one of those very sentimental people who tend to keep empty perfume bottles and jam jars, just in case they may be useful one day. And I have a weakness for pretty scraps of fabric and wrapping paper.

Thanks to all these bits and pieces, I have perfected the fine art of whipping up last-minute school projects and crafty creations, usually with zero notice and no purchases necessary. I think of it as my Superpower. The kids would come rushing through the door: 'Mum, I need a ... (whatever it was for that day) ... by tomorrow!' And somehow, we'd create the requested model, or outfit or creature in a flash.

I blame it on growing up during the years of rations and shortages. Nothing was thrown away. Every jar, ribbon and oddly shaped cardboard insert had a second life waiting for it. It was survival... mine, anyway. So now, my instinct is always: 'Don't toss it ... one day, we'll need it.' And more often than not... we do.

I had entire shelves dedicated to keepsakes. 'Mum gave me that when I turned 12,' or 'That was a leftover from my wedding dress material,' or 'I'll need that for a future dress-up box.' Every item had a story. And I must confess, after seven moves (across farms, cities and eventually countries), I still have my wedding cake icing roses. Yes – the actual sugar icing. All three delicate, handcrafted tiers. How they've survived is anyone's guess, but they've arrived undamaged every single time. I probably do need therapy

... for that one at least. In my next life, I aspire to be a minimalist! But this isn't the life for it.

So, there we were, trying to pack up not only a home, but a life. Harare had become our base, but I knew deep down that soon that house would also have to be packed up too. I was constantly juggling with decisions about what to take, what to store, what to sell and what we needed *right now*. I'd pack something, then promptly unpack it the next day when one of the kids needed it.

PACK IT UP

I was an emotional mess. The reality was hitting home hard. The garden I'd poured so much love into – the roses, the orchids, the waterfall and rockery – was like leaving part of myself behind. I remember weeping when a perfect stranger had arrived to purchase my orchids. The poor woman didn't know what to do with me, a blubbering mess as I handed over the flowers. Of all the things to weep over! I had simply reached breaking point. It wasn't only the plants. It was the end of everything we had built.

At the end of the day, I knew it was all just 'stuff.' I kept telling myself that. But detaching from it was hurting. I needed to shift from clinging to letting go, and even though I understood that in theory, in practice it was extremely difficult.

While I was battling my way through all the boxes and all the memories, Johnny was doing his best to salvage what he could from the farm. So much had already been stolen; tractors, tools, even irrigation equipment. If we didn't move it quickly, we'd lose the lot.

It became increasingly difficult to move things to town, so we took to sending the lorry under cover of darkness, hoping to avoid roadblocks and searches. It was a gamble every time. Equipment we'd bought with our own hard-earned money was suddenly claimed as 'theirs.' They had seized our land, and therefore they considered that everything on the land was theirs too. Even the crops we'd planted and were waiting to harvest were now being claimed by the 'so-called' new owners.

Absolute madness.

That said, we were luckier than most. We managed to shift a fair bit of equipment to Harare, and most of our furniture made it out before it was too late. I'll never forget those strange, chaotic months of sorting, selling, hiding, packing, crying. Basically, doing our best to hold it all together. But somehow, we did.

Our migration agent had promised he'd let us know the minute he received preliminary confirmation of our visa application, so that we could start planning flights and firming up departure dates. At the start of 2002, once all the paperwork had finally been submitted, (Hallelujah!) we were given a date in March for an interview at the Australian Embassy in Harare. We had prepared for this as best we could and felt the interview had gone well. The representative who interviewed Johnny and I, told us that many of the embassy staff had really wanted to handle our case as it was most unusual. Not often did they get nine applications in one sitting! And I suspect that it was lucrative for them as they were paid per application and not per case. We assured her that we wanted to make Australia our home, to live and to die there! She appeared to like that, so we left feeling hopeful. But then began the waiting game.

Those following months became a blur of logistics, forms and endless cardboard boxes. I became an expert in wrapping and learned to make the most awkwardly shaped items fit into the most perfect of spots. We began the process of arranging a shipping container for our belongings. Our friends, also gearing up for the big Aussie leap, fondly called it 'packing for Perth.'

PACK IT UP

At one point, we considered the possibility of travelling to Perth by sea. A ship! Imagine that! We'd have more space, it would be a huge adventure, and maybe we could transport our vehicle that way. But after some investigation, it became abundantly clear that, with passenger ships from South Africa to Perth being few and far between, it was never going to happen. Travel time would have been much longer and, as Johnny tends to get seasick, the idea was vetoed pretty quickly. So, aeroplane it would have to be.

Air travel post-9/11 (it was not even a year after that terrible event, at that point) came with its own set of anxieties, and with our larger than normal brood, we were hunting for the cheapest, yet trustworthy, airline available. We managed to find a few family migration discounts, and since we realised this might be our only chance to travel together as a family for a very long time, we made the bold decision to visit my family in the UK while we waited for the visa to be finalised.

There were no direct flights out of Zimbabwe to either England or Australia, so we planned to drive to Johannesburg, then fly to the UK to visit family there, return to Joburg, and catch up with farming friends (who were already living there after they'd migrated from Zimbabwe themselves), and then say our final farewells to my parents.

Meanwhile, we were living in Harare and slowly clearing out the farm and all the other places where we still had belongings stored. We made trip after trip to Ocean Air Carriers, hauling boxes and crates packed with clothes, crockery, bedding, photo albums, sentimental bits, and that bloody wedding cake icing (of course!) Everything was labelled carefully. Each box had a number and a contents sheet tucked inside so that I could work out exactly what was in which box. Moving a family of nine needed a well-planned system. I also wanted to make sure that heavy boxes with books and the like, were placed at the bottom of the stack to minimise damage.

I also had a special 'everyday' box which was to travel with us, filled with comforting little things like our tea cosy, a couple of familiar mugs, and the kids' pillowcases. I was determined that as soon as we arrived on the other side of the world, in a strange new house, we'd still have a thread of home to hold onto.

One of the first larger items to go into the container was the piano. We had also purchased some new railway sleeper furniture, and after we heard that Western Australia had strict rules on importing wood, we didn't want our old furniture being turned away at the port, so we cleaned and scrubbed what we could to comply with bio-security laws. Our golf clubs and even the treads of all our shoes were cleaned with a toothbrush!

And then came the harder part; where would we stay when we landed in Perth? We knew only a handful of people. There was my cousin Paul, his wife Darrel and their four kids, and two farming families who'd moved a few months ahead of us. So, I reached out to my cousin.

We hadn't really been in much contact at all before then. Poor Paul, Darrel and family!

Imagine suddenly being asked the question, 'Hey guys, can we come and stay? Ummm ... there are nine of us, by the way!'

To my cousins' credit, they didn't hang up on me. I'm not sure how enthralled they were with the whole idea, but their answer was 'Yes!'

18

Farewell

The air tickets were finally issued. Our last farewells had been said, and oh, the tears! We cried rivers. Copious amounts. Enough to soak the goodbye hugs and dampen the photos we pasted into the memory book. Friends had lovingly written their good wishes in there too. We had 'packed for Perth' and this was it; we were off on the biggest adventure of our lives.

The journey began before the sun had stretched across the sky. After a last precious night with dear friends in Harare, we jam-packed the van with our mountains of luggage and bundled in the kids. Saying goodbye was brutally hard. These were not only acquaintances, but the friends who had walked through life with us: the happy times, the tragedies, the many days of tennis and all the ordinary days in between. Those friendships dig deep into your soul, and letting go hurt in a way I can still feel if I close my eyes. But the time had come, and there was no turning back now.

FAREWELL

We drove south towards South Africa but spent the night at 'The Lion and Elephant' motel chalets before tackling the infamous Beitbridge Border at daybreak. Beitbridge could be a nightmare – you never knew whether you'd be through in an hour or stuck there for half the day, depending on which officials served you and the mood they were in at the time. They seemed to enjoy making travellers' lives miserable, with endless searches, picking over every document, eyeing anything they fancied keeping for themselves. Here we were, leaving the country forever, our van crammed with luggage and seven restless kids. Our nerves were stretched as tight as a drum.

Foreign currency was like gold dust in Zimbabwe then, and we had managed to stash some away in clever hiding places. That was the reason our hearts were pounding as we drove up to the barrier, praying silently for a quick and painless crossing. And by some miracle, that's exactly what happened. No real fuss, just a quick and simple search, then a few stamps and we were waved through. The relief was indescribable. Once we were across the Limpopo River and well into South Africa, we pulled over, checked all our banknotes, and, thank heavens, they were still tucked away safely where we'd hidden them. If you ask me quietly, I'll tell you where!

We'd heard horror stories that chilled the blood. One family, desperate to smuggle their forex across the border, had hidden it inside a cuddly toy. Safe, they thought, until they reached the other side and realised the toy was gone. One of the kids had tossed it out of the car window somewhere between Harare and the border. Just imagine; their whole future, scattered on the roadside. That was our nightmare, and it haunted me until I saw our own money safe.

From there, we drove on to Johannesburg and arrived safely at my parents' flat. They lived on the third floor of an apartment block, and space was limited. As usual, out came the mattresses, and we spread the kids across the floor like a camp-out. The older two went to stay with family friends nearby, to spare us the wrath of the caretaker. He always complained when we visited, saying: 'Your children run around so much, bits of ceiling are falling into my teacup!' Poor man, it was probably true, so we thought it best to keep the numbers down.

The plan was to stay there for a week or so, then we would fly to England for a couple of weeks, to spend time with my brothers. My eldest brother Chris and his wife Jane had eleven kids at the time, so their big house would become a lively madhouse with our crew squeezed in too. After that, it was back to Joburg to wait out the visa process. In that time, Johnny would make the long drive back up to Zimbabwe, sell the vehicle, and then fly back down to Joburg to rejoin us. The adventure had truly begun; tears, border nerves, mattresses on the floor and all.

In Joburg we did the rounds, catching up with four or five farming friends who had already made the big leap and settled there. It was comforting really, seeing them coping, carving out new lives, even thriving. This gave us hope that we, too, could manage this whole migration exercise. Nevertheless, it was bittersweet. There was laughter and joy in those reunions, but also that tug of sadness. Who knew when we'd see each other again... if ever.

Then came the moment. We were standing at the airport, bags piled up on trolleys, kids buzzing with excitement, about to check in for the flight to London, when the phone rang. I can still vividly remember it. That call is etched in my memory forever. It was our migration agent Martin, his voice bubbling with the good news – *our visa had been approved!* And not only that, but Johnny, as the main applicant, needed to get to Perth as soon as possible to activate it. WOW! After all those months of planning, second-guessing, agonising over choices, and waiting... finally, the doors had opened. It was happening. We were going to be Aussies.

The journey to England went surprisingly well. The kids behaved beautifully on the flight. Their sheer delight at having their very own little TV screens in the seatbacks kept them entertained for hours. It was a great novelty back then! By the time we landed, though, we were wrung out emotionally and utterly exhausted. Thankfully, there at the airport were Chris and Jane, all smiles, ready to bundle us into their people-mover. And what a people-mover it was, practically a bus! Their Ford Transit could seat sixteen people, which was just as well because, with our brood joining their eleven kids, we now had eighteen kids under one roof. And you know what? Unless someone had told you, you'd never have guessed. The chaos melted into laughter, games and the kind of cousin-bonding that warms the heart.

Those weeks were a whirlwind of family outings and visits. Old friends who had left Zimbabwe for England came to visit, too. Yet more emotional hellos and goodbyes packed into every day. However, looming over it all was the urgent business of getting Johnny to Australia. The morning after our arrival, we were out scouring for the cheapest flight we could find. The only bargain route was through Bali, but with the horrific Rock Café bombing of the Australian soccer team still fresh in everyone's minds, we quickly decided against that.

Instead, we grabbed the next best option on a different route. Within twenty-four hours of arriving in England, Johnny was on another plane, heading for Perth. It was dizzying – a crazy storm of kids, noise, tickets, and tears, but it had to be done.

Whilst Johnny was away in Australia finalising the visa, I wasn't about to sit idle. With Felicity, just a toddler at the time, on my hip, I set off on my own little adventure. We flew up to Aberdeen, where I stopped in to visit my dear friend Kirsty and her husband, and their little baby boy. From there, the plan was to make my way to Papa Stronsay in the Orkney Islands, a proper expedition! That was where my four brothers lived, as monks in the monastery. It felt like a pilgrimage of sorts, not merely a visit, and I was determined to get there.

And so, Felicity and I set off on the next leg, a long bus ride up to Thurso, winding through Inverness and Wick. It felt like one of those journeys that would never end. By the time we finally clambered off that bus, I was more than ready for the ferry. Little did I know that the ferry would be an adventure in itself.

Felicity was eighteen months old, and that's when I discovered, much to the horror of both of us, that she suffered from seasickness. Within no time at all, I was 'wearing' everything she'd eaten. And, of course, there's no such thing as an easy clean-up on a Scottish ferry crammed full of noisy, half-drunken labourers. I can laugh about it now, but at the time, I was utterly mortified. Somehow, though, we survived the crossing and made it into Kirkwall on the mainland late at night. To my huge relief, Brother Gerard (my brother) met us there. We were grateful to spend the night on Orkney mainland with a kind friend of the monastery.

Having my brother with us felt like a gift after all that solo travel. Together we boarded another ferry (mercifully, Felicity's tummy behaved this time) to Whitehall on Stronsay Island. It was an approximate two-hour ferry trip to where, at last, we had a little house waiting for us.

Just when I thought we had surely reached the end of our ferry-hopping marathon, the following day brought one more boat ride, this time in the smallish monastery boat, across to Papa Stronsay itself, where Golgotha Monastery stood.

I can assure you, this type of travel is not for the faint-hearted. It takes grit to cope with the long distances, the waiting, the endless ferries, the cold winds whipping at your face. (It's incredibly windy.) You may have heard of the 'Orkney Walk' – the way in which everyone hunches over, fighting the wind when walking. But oh, was it worth it, to walk into that monastery and see my brothers, living their lives, working and praying, so far away from all we knew.

FAREWELL

The islands are beautifully green, and thankfully it was summertime for our visit, so we took a few walks, sometimes down to the beach. But I wasn't game for a dip in that icy cold North Sea.

The visit was truly moving for me. All the chaos, all the exhaustion, all the sick-stained jumpers were forgotten.

And then suddenly, while staying in that little house on the mainland, the phone rang. It was Johnny. His voice carried across the miles, brimming with excitement: 'G'day Sheila, you're an Aussie, mate!'

We had finally got there!

The trek back to England was as long and arduous as the journey there, but my heart was so light it hardly mattered. Johnny flew back a couple of days after Felicity and I returned, and we had a handful of days together in England before it was time to head back to South Africa for the big leap to Perth. But first, as if he hadn't done enough global travelling already, Johnny had one last mission. He had to drive our van all the way back to Zimbabwe to sell it. The buyer was lined up, fortunately, and as soon as the handover was done, Johnny was straight back on a plane to Joburg, so that we could all catch our flight to Perth. We were all together again.

Those final moments on African soil were bittersweet. The hardest goodbye of all was to my dear parents. The only consolation was the promise that they would visit us in Perth as soon as they possibly could. And, as it turned out, their first visit came four months later, when they came for a reunion with Mum's sister from Canada, who would be visiting my Uncle Bob and all his family living in Perth. That was wonderful for them; the two sisters had not seen each other or their brother for decades. It was wonderful for us too, because we hadn't seen Aunty Cassie since she'd left to live in Canada.

In the meantime, Johnny had already paved the way for us in Perth. On his visa-stamping dash he'd met up with Paul and Darrell and prepared them for the storm that was about to descend; our gang of nine, heading their way.

They were incredibly generous, welcoming us all into their home, and even helping us look for a car; a big people-mover, of course – it had to be. They also helped to make our visa application work, with some business ideas, and helping us get our kids booked into schools for the new year. They were wonderfully kind to us. However, I suspect that after a fortnight with our loud, hungry mob, they were motivated to help us find our own place to rent!

19

Escape Artist

Finding a rental house turned into a huge saga. As soon as landlords heard we had seven kids, it was a polite but firm 'no thanks.' I can't say I blamed them – if the shoe were on the other foot, I might've done the same! We started applying for places that allowed pets, hoping it might indicate a more relaxed attitude. Eventually, we found a landlord who took pity on us. He'd grown up in a big family himself and decided to 'give us a chance.' We rented that house for six months, and at the end of our tenancy, the owners suggested they buy another, bigger property for us to rent from them again. Clearly, they felt their decision to rent to us had been a good one for them. We did our best to look after it and keep it spotlessly clean.

While waiting for the container to arrive, we lived with borrowed essentials and expertly scavenged the rest from roadside 'bulk rubbish' collections. My cousin would drive us around the suburbs that had scheduled pick-ups (the more upmarket the better), eyes peeled for the goldmines.

To a Zimbabwean, it was like walking through a magical land where people just left perfectly fine furniture, toys, household and white goods on the side of the road ... all for free.

One of the first 'treasures' we found was a large and fully functioning microwave oven. It served us faithfully for ten years before we finally put it back out on our own verge for bulk collection. It was still working, by the way. All the memories came flooding back when someone stopped at our verge to pick it up, along with so many other tossed-out items of ours. Full circle.

We cleared the container ourselves when it arrived in Fremantle about six weeks after we arrived in Australia. Miraculously, only a handful of items were damaged; an antique teacup from 1900 and some pieces of the railway sleeper furniture. Not bad at all, considering how many possessions we'd packed and the miles of ocean they had travelled across.

After all, we had been through, the chaotic logistical challenges, the endless farewells to friends and family, we had made it to this place, all nine of us, with a mountain of memories and an amazing story to tell.

Before very long, we were able to call ourselves Australian. But to get to that point, we first had to meet our visa requirements as permanent residents, two full years of running our own business. Our daily ritual became scouring the newspaper classifieds and business-for-sale ads, searching for anything that looked remotely manageable. Every time something interesting popped up, we were off to meet with agents, pore over financial reports and try to picture ourselves in that business. We must've driven through every suburb in Perth, even a few rural towns and one interstate trip, chasing that elusive 'perfect fit.'

We looked at all sorts of ventures from cafés to cleaning companies, newsagents, service stations, butcheries... you name it. We had a massive file full of documents to show for it. But in the end, we settled on a sports shop that had passed our due diligence. We figured, since sport was such a big part of our lives, and the kids were constantly needing uniforms and gear anyway, it made perfect sense. And so 'The Sports Shop' became ours.

That same week, we also bought our home. Talk about diving in headfirst. The shop had been run completely manually, so we decided to modernise it. We did away with the handwritten ledgers and brought in computers. Every single item had to be scanned and uploaded – a mammoth task that took endless late nights of bar coding and labelling everything, right down to each dart flight. We got it done, though.

Those first two years were tough. Between getting the kids to school, running the shop seven days a week, plus late nights on Thursdays, and trying to keep some sense of order at home, we were utterly exhausted. Johnny, ever the outdoorsman, grew frustrated being stuck behind a counter, and it certainly wasn't the financial success we'd hoped for. But, as always, we pressed on. It served its purpose, and we managed to tick every box for our business visa. We finally applied for citizenship, and it was granted, which brought immense relief.

We attended a function hosted by our Shire, where we were awarded our certificates with great pomp and ceremony, and we were also gifted a little gum tree to plant. We stood alongside other families who had also just become Aussies, all singing the Australian anthem together in chorus. It was a very moving evening. The overwhelming culmination of many years of uncertainty, emotional exhaustion, frustration and even flashes of anger and serious depression (on my part).

But we had done it!

We didn't have our friends and family there to celebrate with us in person, but we still felt monumental relief and joy. At last, we could be proud of what we'd achieved. No more living on a visa with conditions and requirements hanging over our heads. We were citizens now. True blue Aussies. We could even apply for passports (and there'd be no risk of Liverpool mysteriously turning up on our paperwork ever again). It was the best feeling in the world to know our family now had a safety net to catch us, if anything happened to one of us. A far cry from the constant insecurity we'd known as Zimbabwean citizens.

Life moved on, and the kids threw themselves into Australian culture. After the initial adjustment to a schooling system with more relaxed rules and less discipline, they settled happily into their own phases of life.

We felt blessed to have had the chance to start over in Perth. That said, there were some really tough financial years. There were times when a family meal out was only possible with trade dollars, and it became the norm to shop at thrift stores or at the supermarket at the end of the day when the mark-downs happened. We were fortunate to have some very generous friends who silently stepped in when we couldn't see a glimmer of light at the end of the tunnel.

A funny little story from that tough period was about the second-hand socks we'd managed to get as part of the kids' school uniforms. The only problem? There were only nine socks, instead of five pairs. So, every morning turned into a mad dash to the wash basket, everyone hoping to grab two socks that were at least vaguely matching and, most importantly, dry. No one wanted to be the one stuck with the inevitable single damp sock, cold and clammy against their toes all day. Oh, the groans through the house when someone lost that sock race!

One of the very first incidents in the rental house was certainly memorable. Amusing in hindsight, but it was terrifying at the time for the kids.

It was one Sunday after Mass. We'd dropped the kids home and then gone back to church for a discussion about schooling options. About half an hour later, I heard my phone ringing. Thank goodness I hadn't put it on silent mode, as I usually did. It was Daniel.

The call went something like this:

'Hi Mum, Felicity has cut herself and there's blood everywhere. Renée has fainted, and I called the ambulance!'

'Ahhh, no! My goodness, what happened? Is she OK?'

'Well, I've put a bandage on it and I'm holding it really tight.'

'Ok, just hang on. Dad and I will be home as soon as we can!'

I informed Johnny about the unfolding situation at home, and we tore off. In my head, I was already imagining the worst ... that her finger had been chopped clean off.

As we were heading home, we suddenly saw an ambulance, siren blaring, racing in the same direction as us. My heart nearly stopped. 'That's it! That's our ambulance!' My panic levels went through the roof.

I called the kids. It sounded like chaos! They were running around like headless chooks, while Paul and André were jumping around nervously in the driveway waiting for the ambulance's grand arrival.

Then, two roads from home, we passed another ambulance, also sirens wailing, but this one turned off in a different direction to our house. Again, I thought, well, maybe that's our ambulance and it's lost?

Finally, we screeched into the driveway. As we dashed inside, we saw Daniel sitting with Felicity on his lap. She wasn't crying. In fact, she looked quite happy with herself. Daniel, however, was seriously stressed and had wads of tissue wrapped around her tiny finger, soaked through with blood. He was holding it up in the air like some kind of flag of victory.

I immediately realised that there was no ambulance needed here. I rang quickly to see if I could cancel it and explained with much embarrassment, 'There's been panic and rather an overreaction from my children. I'm really sorry for the inconvenience!'

The poor emergency operator must have thought we were quite mad. Thankfully, the ambulance had only just been dispatched and was easily cancelled. That Sunday seemed to have been an 'ambulance emergency' day, judging by the number of ambulances we'd seen and heard.

Back inside, I dealt with the finger. Renée had come round but still looked rather woozy. I tried to peek under Daniel's heroic 'tissue bandage,' but her fingers were so tiny I worried that I'd open up the cut again. Better to be safe. We bundled Felicity into the car, and we drove, more slowly this time, straight back down the freeway, half an hour, to the children's hospital, near to the church where we'd been earlier. It was our third trip for the day to that part of town.

The nurse gently removed Daniel's mountain of tissue and revealed a deep cut across the top of her little index finger. Any deeper, and she might have chopped it off. Her fingertip was too small for stitches, so they taped it firmly, dressed it, and sent us home. It healed beautifully in time, leaving only the faintest scar, one only those who know the story will ever notice.

So, what had actually happened? It turned out that the kids were all eating apples, and naturally, Felicity wanted one too. Miss Independent grabbed a knife and decided to peel and cut it all by herself. A toddler, a knife and an apple can only equate to inevitable disaster. She didn't even really cry (a family trait, this high pain threshold), she just called out, 'I'm bleeding!' Blood had started to pour everywhere, onto the floor, onto the Lego where she and her brothers were playing, onto anything in range.

Paul called out to Renée, (the 'adult' in the room). As the eldest, she had taken on the role as second Mum whenever we had errands to do and had to leave the kids alone. She instantly began to shout orders. 'Get something to hold onto it, stop the bleeding!' Paul dashed off and returned with a roll of tissue. 'No! That will stick!' Off he went again, coming back with a towel. 'Too big, it needs to be wet,' she cried.

Daniel, being very literal, took Felicity to the bathroom and ran the wound under the tap instead of wetting the towel, so now blood was pouring out like a fountain and all over the sink. Renée took one look and promptly keeled over. She has always been a fainter at the sight of blood.

Imagine the scene: Daniel in full-blown panic, Felicity still not crying, Monique watching in horror as her 'big sister' lay flat out on the bathroom floor and her 'little sister' was apparently bleeding to death. Daniel quickly wrapped wads of tissue, at least half the roll, around Felicity's finger. Then he decided it was all far too serious and, not knowing what else to do, he called the ambulance. As you do!

All's well that ends well. Although, whenever I see Felicity peel an apple, I get a little twitchy.

We had another nerve-wracking incident while we were still renting that house, and my parents were visiting us for the first time since we moved to Perth.

Johnny and I had left early that morning on yet another of the many 'business hunting' expeditions. We dropped the two older kids at Prendiville College on the way to meet a business sales agent and left my parents in charge of the younger ones.

Our rental was within walking distance of the junior school, so each morning, without fail, the kids were walked there. At the time, Paul, André, and Monique were in primary school, Philip was in pre-kindergarten, and little Felicity was still a toddler. As usual, my parents walked the kids to their classrooms, and they then walked back home afterwards.

Mum went off to have a bath and Dad busied himself with the dishes. Mum assumed Felicity was pottering about with Dad. Dad assumed Felicity was keeping Mum company. After a while, the house was much too quiet. Dad realised he couldn't hear the usual toddler chatter or mischief. That prickly feeling set in and he went to check.

The side gate was latched. No sign of Felicity. He called her name, then asked Mum if she had her, only to find out Mum had been in the bath the whole time. His stomach dropped.

Panic.

They searched everywhere, every room, every cupboard, the garden, the street... but no Felicity. Just as they were about to call the police (and us!) the phone rang. It was the school.

We hadn't been in Australia for long, and the school community didn't know us very well yet. Someone had spotted Felicity sitting in the sandpit at the school playground, playing happily. That parent had simply assumed this little girl's mum or dad was nearby. Luckily, someone I knew from Philip's pre-kindy class recognised her as Pip's little sister and realised she hadn't seen me at the class drop off that morning. She asked around and went to the reception, as no one had seen either Johnny or I at the school, they decided to call our house.

When Mum took the call and heard Felicity was safe, she and Dad raced back to the school. To this day, we have no idea how she got out and re-latched the gate behind herself. Somehow, that determined little girl had crossed a double-laned road and found her way straight to the playground. Obviously, she had remembered where her big brothers and sister spent their mornings.

My parents waited until we returned from our day's 'business hunt' to tell us what had transpired. They'd been sick with worry but decided there was no point in making us panic too, since she was already home safe.

Just when we thought that was the end of Felicity's escapades, she struck again. On this occasion, we were all busy inside, each of us assuming someone else was keeping an eye on her. She quietly slipped out the front door, wandered down the street, and was spotted eventually by a kind neighbour who guessed, correctly, that the noisy house full of kids must be where she belonged. There was a knock at the door, and I opened it to find a man holding Felicity in his arms, telling us he'd rescued her from the road. With huge embarrassment, I thanked him for being so kind and thoughtful.

That was my wake-up call. We were very lucky to be living in a neighbourhood where people looked out for each other. Both incidents could have ended so differently. The rental wasn't an ideal location for a toddler because the front door faced the road, the garage opened straight onto it, and there was no fence to keep the children in, or anything else out.

Felicity, it turned out, was not only our youngest... she was also our resident escape artist!

One day, toward the end of our time running The Sports Shop, right around when we finally gained our Australian citizenship, a customer hung around for a chat. It's strange how a simple conversation can change the direction of your life. That casual chat led to a big decision. We closed the doors on retail and opened a whole new chapter in garden landscaping.

Johnny was in his element again, back outdoors. It wasn't farming exactly, but it was close enough to make his heart happy. There was something about working with his hands in the soil that seemed to bring him back to himself. That little leap of faith turned out to be one of the best decisions we ever made. The business became our mainstay, steady and reliable, and it helped us turn our finances and our spirits around. In reflection, it feels like the land has always had a way of calling Johnny home, no matter where we are.

My parents visited every few years when they could afford the trip, and those visits brought so much joy that our hard times faded quickly in memory. The kids all built strong friendships through their school years, bonds that many of them still maintain today. They enjoyed opportunities that I honestly doubt they would have had if we'd stayed in Zimbabwe. Careers and paths none of us could have imagined back then. Renée met her future husband, Gareth, and along the way, we've gathered a circle of like-minded Australian friends who have become part of our story.

20

Four Missing Decades

After Johnny's dad passed away in 2008, his half-sister Anna, began reaching out to all her brothers and sisters scattered across the globe. Out of that came something none of us had dared to dream. Johnny was finally able to speak to his family in Venezuela. He hadn't seen or spoken to his mum, his older sister Laurinda, or Antonio (his youngest brother) for over thirty-nine years! Nearly four decades of silence, and suddenly, here was the chance to change that.

The phone calls began almost the very moment we got the numbers from Anna. I can still feel the emotional energy when Johnny made that first call. I had wondered how they would communicate and whether they would even be able to understand him. I could see his nerves and excitement swirling together.

Suddenly, it happened. Antonio answered the call. In that instant Johnny's whole face lit up, his smile wide, his eyes shining, as if a missing piece of himself had just been returned. Then, his mother was handed the phone. The moment he heard her say his name, everything inside him seemed to break wide open. His face just crumpled, and the tears started streaming down his face in pure joy. The sound of his voice when he said 'Mãe!' (Mum.) I don't think I will ever forget that. It was one of those moments so raw and real that it has been stored in my memory bank forever.

Of course she was completely overwhelmed, as we all were. None of us could quite believe what was unfolding before us, especially after all those long, silent years, desperately waiting for this connection to happen. It felt surreal, as if time had disappeared in that moment; oceans, decades, and heartache were somehow bridged with that phone call.

When Laurinda's turn came, her voice seemed familiar to him. The moment was thick with emotion, and the tears streamed again. It was almost impossible to get the words out. With every new voice Johnny heard that night, another missing piece of his heart seemed to find its way home.

It wasn't easy. After so long in Venezuela, their Portuguese seemed to have been replaced by Spanish, so there was a fair bit of 'umming' and laughing, in desperation at the inability to find the words at first. But by the end of that first long chat, the Portuguese started flowing again, albeit slowly from Johnny's end. There were tears, laughter and endless stories. The years seemed to melt away. Before long, the calls moved to Skype, and suddenly, we weren't just hearing them all, we were seeing them. The first time Johnny saw his mother's face after thirty-nine years, his hand went straight to his mouth, and I could see the tears rolling.

Then came the plan, a secret mission. Johnny would fly to Venezuela. He wanted it to be a surprise for his mother. In early June 2009, Johnny made his way to Venezuela. No one told his mother, so she had absolutely no idea. I still get goosebumps thinking about it. Incidentally, the day he left Perth, news broke about the Air France flight from Rio that had gone down in the Atlantic Ocean. My heart was in my throat as the incident was shown on TV. Johnny was heading to that part of the world right as I was watching it unfold over the news. Thankfully, this wasn't going to be another one of his near-death stories.

The family worried their mother might not survive the shock, as after all, she'd said goodbye twice already, first to her boy when he was just twelve, and then after hearing false reports, had mourned him as if he'd died. And now, to see him alive, standing in the kitchen? How would she cope with that?

The suspense-filled moment came. She was at the fridge, pulling something out, turned around to close the door and there he was. She screamed, thinking he must be a burglar! She was completely oblivious and knew nothing of the surprise awaiting her. Laurinda rushed in, laughing and crying and explaining. It was only then the realisation hit her. The shock was huge, and they needed to sit her down and calm her. How could she possibly be seeing her son right there, in front of her! She clutched Johnny, and dissolved into sobs, unable to let him go. He was a crying mess too; he'd been in tears of joy since landing earlier that day. After two days of emotional travel, reuniting with his siblings at the airport, and now seeing his mother after nearly four decades, it was almost too much to bear.

The house was filled with people, as the extended family gathered together to witness this monumental reunion. Cameras were capturing the precious moments; everyone was crying and laughing at once. It was chaos... but the most beautiful chaos you can imagine. I so wished I could have been there to witness it all.

Those four weeks in Venezuela were a complete whirlwind for Johnny. We had only ever heard about his nieces and nephews, and suddenly, there they were in front of him. They chatted about all the stories from the missing years, filling in the gaps of a life only imagined from afar. Every day brought more visits and introductions from extended family. The resemblance between our kids and Antonio's and Laurinda's was uncanny. Familiar smiles, gestures and expressions.

Johnny and his brother Antonio clicked instantly, despite the years of separation. Weirdly sharing the same cheeky humour as if they'd never been apart. Antonio resembled their dad the most in looks, though certainly not in character.

When he came home, I noticed something new within Johnny; a deep, restored bond with his family. He'd filled in most of the missing pieces of his own history, and finally, after so many years separated from his mother, Laurinda and Antonio, whilst he was living in Zimbabwe, that invisible thread which had almost snapped, was now being sewn back into something strong. It was truly special.

Antonio and the family also managed to arrange for José, the eldest of the siblings, to make the journey to Venezuela the year after Johnny's visit. It was a great pity they couldn't all have been there at the same time. It would have been an extraordinary reunion. It was almost as if Filomena's prayer was answered in two parts. She had longed to see her two sons again, and though not at the same time, she was blessed with the joy of holding each of them after so many years of separation. For her, it was a dream fulfilled, a piece of her heart mended.

José's separation had been even longer than Johnny's, so his visit was particularly precious, both for his mother and for the rest of the family who had been waiting so long to embrace him. They treasured the time as though it might never come again. It never did.

I have a lingering sadness that I was never able to meet Johnny's brother José in person, not once. It's a missing piece in the family puzzle, and I know his story only through the tales and memories of others.

September of that same year was a whirlwind of joy and family reunions. Renée and Gareth were married, which was an occasion tucked in my heart forever. My parents travelled to Perth for the event, and my brother, Father Anthony Mary, came over from the Monastery in order to celebrate the nuptial Mass. That alone made the day extra special. Renée's godparents, Chris and Jane, my eldest brother and sister-in-law, were also there to celebrate the occasion.

It was a flying visit for them in more ways than one. They had to dash straight back to the UK because their daughter, my goddaughter, was getting married only two weeks later. Of course, my parents were going to that wedding too, so it became a sort of 'wedding safari' for my folks. Two countries, two granddaughters' weddings, all in two weeks!

That UK trip turned out to be bittersweet. Tragically, it was the last time my beautiful mother would travel. She'd taken ill on the final flight home to South Africa from the UK and needed to go straight from the airport to the hospital. Towards the end of their stay in England, she began to feel sick. Her finger had accidentally been closed in the car door at Perth airport as they were about to leave for the UK, and I now wonder whether this was the cause of it all. She developed septicaemia and was treated in hospital for this. Mum rallied, but other things started to go wrong with her. Dad believed she would be fine, but instinctively I knew I had to get there as soon as I could.

I booked the trip, never imagining it would end the way it did. When I arrived, she appeared to be turning the corner. We played cards and her favourite, 'Rummikub' together in her hospital room. She was laughing and chatting, although her breathing was still slightly laboured. The specialist did his rounds on Wednesday morning, and since he was satisfied with her progress, he told us she could go home at last. Her whole face lit up. That was all she had wanted – to be back in her own home.

Father Anthony managed to make the journey there to be with Mum too, which meant the world to her. One of the great joys of my parents' life was attending daily Mass, so for Mum to have her own priest son say Mass in her room each day after she had returned from hospital was a huge comfort.

To everyone's relief, she appeared to improve and by Friday she was able to walk a little and sit up in the lounge. One of the neighbours popped in and had tea with her. We had no idea that this would be the last day she would leave her bed.

I will always count it as one of the greatest blessings of my life that I was with my mum when she slipped away on that Saturday morning, 12th December 2009. Unimaginable considering how bright she had looked only the day before. By strange coincidence, it was the same date as my brother Basil's birthday. Father Anthony was nearing the end of Mass. Mum had just received the Blessed Eucharist in Holy Communion. She had whispered her quiet thanksgiving, told us she loved us, and then, with a completely peaceful expression on her face, simply let go. We were right there with her and had no idea at the start of Mass that it would end like that.

It was devastating for all of us – Dad, Father Anthony and I – but it was also indescribably beautiful. A holy passing. Another moment I hold forever my heart.

What a year it had been.

21

Filling in the Blanks

On the trip that Johnny made to Venezuela to meet up with his family for the first time in four decades, and on each subsequent visit to Madeira, we were able to add more and more parts to the puzzle. By the end, we could piece together how things really had played out all those years ago.

Johnny's dad had left the island around 1965, and life simply had to go on without him. It wasn't easy for his family. In fact, it was brutally hard. With no steady income, they struggled to put food on the table. As soon as Antonio was old enough, he took whatever odd jobs he could, but most days, there simply wasn't enough to eat. Many days, Antonio was starving.

Then came the story that no one wanted to bring up. We'd heard whisperings but didn't know it all. Filomena, desperate to keep her children fed, found herself in an impossible situation. She made a choice no woman should ever have to make. She resorted to trading what little she had left to give, in order to get food. This was entirely an act of survival, but of course, it was never going to end well. Inevitably, she became pregnant.

In a place as small as Madeira, secrets never stayed secret for long, and word of the pregnancy travelled fast on the island. And, as gossip does, the news eventually reached her husband José far away in Rhodesia. He was furious when he heard this news, although, in honesty, he hadn't been around to support his family, and as everyone knew, nor had he been particularly faithful himself. Morality aside, desperation forces desperate choices to be made.

The pregnancy, sadly, ended in a stillbirth. As heartbreaking as it was, perhaps it was also a small mercy given the tangled family circumstance.

By 1979, Laurinda had left Madeira for Venezuela to join her husband, José. Together, they successfully ran a supermarket. Their family grew to four children.

Antonio and his mother followed Laurinda to Venezuela in 1980. Antonio married Maria, who had tragically lost her husband in a terrible accident. She had two daughters when Antonio married her, and then together, they had a son and daughter.

Antonio had a very successful bakery, and things were going well for both families until Venezuela's economy began to collapse, and with it, the life they had all built there.

After years battling financial struggles, they all finally left Venezuela. Antonio and his family, along with his mother, settled in Spain, and Laurinda and her family found their way to Portugal.

Meanwhile, back in Africa, José, Johnny's father, was still hopelessly in love with Katarina. Now that Filomena was out of Madeira, he saw his chance. He could take Katarina with him to South Africa and marry her there. The laws were different in Africa, and it was far removed from questioning by the inquisitive locals in Ribeira Grande. So, in 1981, Katarina packed her bags and left the island with José.

Very soon after her arrival in South Africa, she fell pregnant, which was a huge blessing for her. She'd faced some serious health challenges and, already into her late forties, wasn't sure if she'd ever be able to conceive the child she hoped for. Then along came Anna, her miracle baby, in 1982.

At Katarina's insistence, José began saving every bit of profit from their shop and sending it back to Madeira, little by little, to build a house. A home they could return to in their old age, should they ever leave South Africa – which, in time, they did.

With each return to the island, they'd bring a few more treasures with them; furniture, fittings, keepsakes – and they added a little more to the build. In just a few short years, a beautiful home had been carved right into the side of the mountain, standing proudly beside the church.

It was in that house, built with so much skill, determination and love, that we stayed on our honeymoon. Even today, it still stands strong, a testament to their hard work and the life they had built together.

However, with each visit back to Madeira, there was no escaping the unspoken history. Everyone who knew the family also knew that José had walked away from his wife and children… and then married his sister-in-law. And there was beautiful little Anna, blameless in every way, born from the affair, but with no say about how she came into the world.

Naturally, her loyalty lay with her parents, but she wasn't blind to the undercurrents. She could feel the tension, see the glances, and sometimes even hear the sharp, unkind remarks. Most of the time, she kept to herself.

Now, as an adult, she understands it all more clearly; the layers of hurt, the tangled loyalties. Living right next door to the family who have carried the burden of her arrival into their lives, a constant reminder of those old wounds. Life in Madeira has never been simple for her and never without its awkwardness.

To those who knew how hard Johnny's father had been on his family, it was an incomprehensible truth that, despite everything, they still loved him.

After Mum passed away, Dad tried to travel as much as he could, doing his best to escape the icy Johannesburg winters. He would divide up his year of travel, spending about six months in Joburg, then three months here in Australia (the maximum they'd allow on a visitor's visa), and another three months in the UK with my eldest brother and his family. He loved being with the kids and grandkids. It gave him purpose and joy.

One of those trips coincided with the birth of Renée and Gareth's first child, Mikey – his first great-grandchild. It turned into quite a saga. It was Good Friday, and Dad managed to do himself an injury in the most ridiculous way possible, while putting his trousers on. He put his foot on the fabric of the trouser leg and slipped with his knee buckling backwards under him. True to form, stoical, stubborn and determined not to be a bother, Dad brushed it off. 'Just a bit sore,' he said, more annoyed with himself and his clumsiness than anything else.

I knew Dad had a very high pain threshold, (which I believe I have inherited) and an absolute refusal to ever 'make a fuss', but this was a whole new level. On Easter Saturday, he came along with us to visit friends, and all he'd taken for the pain was two Panadol tablets. He sat there, cheerfully chatting, while his leg throbbed away, politely refusing further pain relief.

By Sunday, his knee was the size of a watermelon. He muttered, 'Sore, but not too bad,' and insisted he didn't need anything stronger than another two Panadol. It was only then that I bundled him off to hospital, but everything moved painfully slow, as it was the Easter weekend.

There was an added complication. Decades earlier, Dad had been treated for bowel cancer and had lived with an ileostomy bag ever since. Hours of waiting in that emergency admissions area left him in dire need. My heart broke for him. I'd seen those humiliating situations before, at airports, on car trips, even while out shopping. His bag bursting or leaking without any warning. He would just quietly endure, sometimes having to buy a new pair of trousers on the spot. He bore it all with such grace, but it was a cruel ordeal for such a dignified man.

Back to the knee. Dad needed surgery as he had broken his kneecap and torn some of the tendon off the bone. The stay in hospital turned out to be a dreadful experience for Dad. The hospital was completely full, so he was left lying in an isolation room which unbelievably, had no working air conditioner. With temperatures up to 41 degrees in the shade, no windows and no airflow, my father became dehydrated from perspiring heavily and prolonged fasting as the operation had been postponed twice. It was appalling. Surgery finally took place, but they discharged him only one day later. I did lodge an official complaint afterwards, but of course, nothing came of it.

Consequently, the remainder of Dad's visit was somewhat dampened and a lot less fun. To top it off, he celebrated his 80th birthday, not with a much-loved round of golf, but with a rather unglamorous cast on his leg. He took it all in his stride – so to speak.

There was, however, a silver lining. The injury meant he got to travel 'Business Class' on his journey back home, to accommodate his outstretched leg during the long flight.

Despite it all, Dad healed remarkably well and was soon back on the golf course. He managed his planned UK trip the following year. And would you believe it, he went and broke the other knee there. This time, he simply stood up after reading, but his leg had 'gone to sleep', and as he stepped outside, it gave way beneath him. Two broken knees one year apart. At least he was able to compare the hospital quality between Australia and the UK, and let's just say, the UK hospital won hands down!

The following year, Dad spent a long stint in ICU at hospital following a bowel perforation during a routine procedure. His health deteriorated over the next year and never fully returned. Eventually, we arranged for him to go into a care facility, because he couldn't live alone anymore. But like Mum before him, all he wanted was to be in his own home.

Sadly, he never did get back home. He passed away suddenly after being readmitted to hospital. Neither I nor any of my brothers could get there in time to be with him. It was devastatingly sad to know he died with none of his children present. By another amazing coincidence, he died on Father Anthony's birthday. It is a blessing that my parents both died on the birthday of one of their sons. His funeral enabled me to spend time together with all seven of my brothers, which was a special blessing. A rare gathering of family, in honour of a man who endured so much, complained so little, and somehow always maintained his dignity, even in the most undignified of circumstances.

22

Mum or Bomma

Life in Perth continued, and the family grew. 2012 proved to be a very productive year.

When Renée and Gareth had announced that they would be giving us our first grandchild, we were over the moon. However, I'd had a dream a few months earlier that I too was pregnant. Goodness me, imagine that! Knowing that this was highly unlikely as I was already experiencing symptoms of menopause and was in my forty-fifth year. Our youngest was eleven years old at the time, so I had written off this possibility in my mind.

Maybe my body was simply preparing my mind for what was to come. Imagine our surprise when I visited the doctor and described all my menopausal symptoms ... only to discover that I was in fact pregnant. Unbelievable! The doctor looked astonished and said, 'I think I'm more surprised than you are!'

I walked out of the doctor's rooms, got into the car, and promptly burst into tears. It wasn't so much the shock of the news itself, though that was big enough, but my anxiety about how Johnny was going to take it. How on earth was I going to tell him?

I rang him straight away. As I broke the news, Renée and a few of the other kids happened to be nearby. Johnny told Renée but decided not to tell the others until I was home. He wanted it to be a proper family announcement.

When I walked in later that afternoon, there they all were, just as usual, seated around our big dining table, mugs of tea and snacks spread out after school and work. Johnny, who is not one for public shows of affection unless it's Christmas, a birthday, or some other special occasion, came straight up to me, gave me a kiss and the biggest hug, and beamed from ear to ear. With an enormous grin plastered across his face, he announced, 'Mum has something to tell you all!'

Well, I'll never forget their reactions. They're worth describing because each one is a classic.

Philip, who was thirteen at the time, was the first to speak. 'Oh wow! Did we win the lottery?' (And in a way, we had!) He couldn't fathom why his dad was suddenly so exuberant.

So, I smiled and announced to them all: 'You're going to have another brother or sister!'

André rolled his eyes and said, 'Yeah, we know, Renée's pregnant.'

'No,' I corrected him, '*YOU* are going to have another brother or sister.'

The penny dropped first with Daniel. He looked at me, eyes narrowing, and said slowly, 'Oh right … NO! That's so gross.'

The rest of them stared at each other, puzzled, before the giggles started. Then came the proper laughs, the happy kind that ripple around a table until everyone's caught up in it.

Philip piped up again, 'Oh wow! Awesome, I'm learning about that at school!' Cue my cringe, the kind that only a mother can feel when her thirteen-year-old son makes that connection out loud.

Renée, who was herself five months pregnant at the time, saw the look of worry in my eyes and jumped in. With all the wisdom and grace of someone far beyond her years, she told her dad and all of us that it was wonderful news, and that everything was going to be fine. She really did ease my heart and her dad's too, that day.

Monique and Paul weren't there, so I had to call them both.

Monique's response was identical to André's: 'Yes, I know! Renée's pregnant.'

'No,' I said for the second time that day. '*YOU* are going to have another brother or sister!'

There was a pause before she exclaimed, 'Oh wow, … Renée's having twins?'

'No, Monique,' I said for the third time, laughing by now. '*YOU* are going to have another brother or sister!'

Finally, it clicked. She let out an almighty laugh, complete with some colourful language, and then happily congratulated us.

When I rang Paul, it was almost word for word the same. 'Wait ... what? Renée's having twins!'

'Not Renée,' I said patiently.

There was a silence. Then he spluttered, 'Umm, no way! How is that even possible?' Whether he meant from an age point of view or, well, the obvious other point of view, I wasn't about to ask him to clarify. He came around quickly enough though, and was happy for us too.

In the days that followed, we told family and friends. Almost every single one thought we were joking. The disbelief on people's faces was priceless, but once the shock wore off, everyone gave us their heartfelt congratulations. That helped to calm mine and Johnny's very understandable concerns.

Naturally, I couldn't help feeling I had stolen Renée's thunder. This was supposed to be her season of joy, her first baby, our first grandchild, and suddenly her mother was having baby number eight as a 'granny'. It also meant that she was about to gain another sibling, due only three months after her baby, but twenty-four years younger than her. It was nuts. I'd been rebranded under the delightful medical term 'geriatric pregnancy.' Renée, in her grace, never once made me feel guilty. Instead, she supported me through those long, strange months.

The looks we were given when we were out together, were interesting. You could see people trying to do the mental maths, and the comments were sometimes downright bizarre.

'So, your new baby is going to be an aunt or uncle younger than their niece or nephew?' Yes. 'You're the granny, *AND* you're pregnant?' Some people took a while to wrap their heads around that.

One of the funniest reactions was on the day Renée went into labour. I went with her to the hospital. She introduced me to her gynaecologist, who looked at Renée, and then at me, at her bump and then at mine. The expression on his face when he realised the situation was priceless.

Our beautiful little boy Antonio arrived in 2012 – on the very same day Johnny and I celebrated our twenty-fifth wedding anniversary. Now, that must be the most unforgettable and novel anniversary gift we could ever have given each other. A silver anniversary marked by a brand-new little life. Perfect timing. As if that wasn't special enough, Antonio's grand entrance was just three months after our gorgeous first grandson, Michael, had been born, so he instantly became an uncle.

It was such a joy sharing that season with Renée. We swapped notes and compared nappies like two new mums together, except that I had had a couple of decades' worth of baby experience behind me. Still, after eleven years and now living in a different country, I had to admit that my body had aged, and my patience or energy wasn't as boundless. But when it came to understanding why a baby was crying and the practicalities of getting them to sleep, I had that knowledge in spades. Johnny, almost ten years older than me, and I found ourselves in the most unusual role; grandparents for the first time, yet new parents all over again.

I remember thinking I couldn't quite be the doting 'Bomma' (the Belgian name for Granny that I inherited from my mother, and she from hers), because I was far too busy being Mum all over again.

Life didn't slow down for a second. The boys grew up, side by side, like brothers, while Renée and Gareth added to their tribe with two more boys in quick succession. Before we could catch our breath, Mikey, Oin, and Heath were all running around together; three little boys in just under three years. They all look so different that we often joke they're 'chocolate, strawberry, and vanilla,' thanks to their varying hair colours.

The boys are the best of buddies with Antonio and hang out and have 'sleepovers' as often as they are permitted. Looking from the outside in, it seems a strange dynamic, Antonio calling Renée, his sister, by her name, when the others call her Mum, and Antonio calling me Mum when the other boys call me Bomma. But however strange it seems, this is their 'normal'.

The family expansion didn't stop there. In time, Paul was married, and before long we were blessed with two beautiful granddaughters, Isla and then little Molly. They moved to Sydney, which means our whole noisy crew can't gather as often as we'd love, but oh, when we do, it's a treasured, magical time. André and Chloe too have added darling little Alfie to the growing list of 'grandies' and soon they will have a new baby to dress in pink.

In the middle of all that wonderful chaos, Johnny and I made the big decision to sell our home and find somewhere with a smaller mortgage. It felt like déjà vu; another massive pack-up reminiscent of our farm days. Only this time it was driven by the simple reality that there was always more 'month' left than money. This time, a move by choice and not by force.

Just like before, our friends rallied, boxes were packed, and we landed in our new place. A 'shed' or, as it is affectionately known now, 'The Block'. It's a rural, peaceful, and much larger property, so, although we referred to the move as 'downsizing', in truth it gave us much more breathing space than before, especially financially. Rural living always brings its own set of challenges, like no internet for six months and relying on the rain to fill the water tank. The ticks, the kangaroos eating the flowers, the foxes eating the chickens, constant power-outages and very poor phone and internet signal. But despite it all, we've grown to love living here.

23

End of an Erra – not a spelling error

Throughout those busy years, Johnny and I managed a few more trips. This was all courtesy of our son, Daniel. He was working as an Aircraft Engineer for an airline and was able to book significantly cheaper flights for us. One of the first and most memorable was flying back to Tiaseka, our old farm in Zimbabwe. That visit was something I'll never forget.

Walking through what had once been our paradise was surreal. The lush gardens, the aviaries, the chapel, the beautiful house, all of it had been stripped away. Where roses had bloomed, an ox plough now sat rusting. The wooden parquet floors and staircases were gone, burnt for firewood. The swimming pool was a cracked, empty cement shell. Every room had soot stains around the broken windows, where fires had been lit. I think each room must have housed a family or more. And the attic room, the very one where Philip had been hidden during the day of that terrifying farm invasion, was now home to a herd of goats!

It should have broken our hearts. Yes, the shock was real and the disappointment sharp, but strangely, both Johnny and I felt unemotional. We stood there, shocked at what lay before us, remembering what had once been. Yet, we were strangely calm. Perhaps enough years had passed, perhaps the memories had already been laid to rest. It was also a dose of reality for Johnny. Until then, he had still harboured faint hopes of returning to farm there. But now, these ideas were firmly blotted out. I wasn't bitter; I was simply curious. Curious to see what had become of the farm stolen from us. That other life, that other time.

We returned home to Perth and plodded on with the busyness and normality of our lives and work. We were very excited when we finally made plans to visit Johnny's family. I was especially desperate to meet Johnny's mother, Filomena Erra, a woman about whom I had heard so much; someone I admired deeply even without having met her. Johnny, Antonio and I were booked on flights for June 2020. It was going to be a special trip. Antonio (our son) would meet his godparents for the first time: Tio Antonio, Johnny's brother, and Tia Laurinda, his sister. After Spain and Portugal, we'd carry on to the UK to visit my side of the family too.

And then suddenly the world turned upside down. Covid hit, borders slammed shut, and all our carefully laid plans evaporated overnight. I told myself there would surely be time later, when Covid restrictions eased up. But the craziness never seemed to have an end. Time is a very fragile thing. Johnny's mother grew more frail after suffering a stroke, and before we could get there, very sadly she slipped away in November 2021, right in the thick of the pandemic. It was simply not to be. This loss sat heavily on our hearts. It was made all the sharper by the fact that I'd never had the chance to sit with her, to look into her eyes, hold her hand or ever hear her voice in person.

In 2023, Johnny received a message that there was some issue with a piece of land in Maroços that had been left to the family. His dad had passed away, and because none of Johnny's full siblings were living on the island anymore, he was asked to go and see whether he could sort it out. It seemed crazy that he, living halfway across the world, should be the one to travel to Madeira. His brother now living in Spain, and his sister living in Portugal were only a stone's throw away, and one would have expected that it would have been closer and easier for them to deal with the problem. They had a much better command of the Portuguese language than Johnny did. José, the eldest and (really) the rightful son to take on this duty, simply couldn't travel. So, Johnny, the helpful peacemaker in the family, decided he would have to go.

Daniel came to the rescue again with cheaper air travel, and thankfully Covid flight restrictions had finally been lifted.

As Johnny had not seen his brother and sister since they'd left Venezuela, he thought he could make his route via Spain, where his brother Antonio and family were now living. The trip was carefully planned out, and the two brothers would drive to Portugal to visit Laurinda and then Johnny would head to Madeira.

However, the best–laid plans often don't work out!

Johnny's chosen travel dates coincided exactly with Pope Francis' apostolic visit to Fatima for World Youth Day – absolutely the worst time to be journeying around Europe, particularly to Spain and Portugal. It turned into something of a disaster. He missed connecting flights, couldn't reach his planned destinations, (they had to drive part of the way) and Johnny ended up paying full fares for last-minute flights, which are never cheap. Fortunately, he was flying alone; with crowded airports and overbooked flights during peak season, it would have been a nightmare for two to navigate that situation.

It was a bittersweet day when Johnny drove with Antonio and his wife down to see Laurinda and her family in the south of Portugal. They were all reunited, having a wonderful big family meal together, when they got word from South Africa that José, their eldest brother, had suddenly passed away. The details were not clear, but it appeared that he had been unwell and, sadly, had died alone. One consolation was that they were together when the news came. Now Johnny was the oldest son, left to deal with the land saga. When he eventually reached Madeira after the crazy travel chaos, he was able to start the process with the knowledge he would have to return later to finish it. The family pleaded for Johnny to bring me and our son, Antonio, along on the next visit.

Roll on one year later.

Antonio and I finally got to meet his godparents for the very first time. It felt almost surreal. Knowing someone through a screen for years is very different from feeling the warmth of a real hug. That moment was truly special. To be meeting this 'missing' part of the family in person at last, and for Antonio, experiencing firsthand the country of his roots; the Portugal his dad had come from and spoken about so often; a land rich with the heritage that shapes who he is.

Our first stop was London. Unfortunately, a few missed connections meant our visit with my UK family was cut short to just one day and a night. That's one of the unfortunate setbacks of staff travel – the chances of being bumped off a flight are always high, especially when there are three of you trying to squeeze into the few available seats. The long layovers, the mad dashes through airports to get to the departure gate in time, the unexpected expenses for last-minute hotels, sometimes it all feels too much. I sometimes wonder if it's really worth it. However, there are the moments when we do get lucky, like an upgrade that makes the journey almost feel glamorous. This is when I remind myself how blessed we are to be able to travel as often as we do... thanks to Daniel.

No doubt there'll be many more journeys ahead, at least we hope so, giving us more precious chances to see as much of our widespread family as possible, while we're still able to. And then, as always, we find ourselves back on 'The Block', slipping into the rhythm and normality of everyday life again, facing its challenges head-on but grateful for the balance between adventure and home.

Lastly, if you ever meet Johnny, you may not notice that he's missing one of his front teeth. His big moustache, that has only once in his life been shaved clean, hides the gap. His laughs and cheeky grins will give it away, so if ever he's captured in a photo with his mouth open, I have spent hours of editing to cut and paste teeth.

It all started back in his army days when he injured himself during a contact as he dived for cover. The MAG whacked him in the mouth, and he had to have some treatment done to stitch up his mouth and lips, repairing his mouth and teeth. This resulted in a permanently discoloured front tooth.

When we first met, that tooth was only slightly darker than the other, and many years later the bottom half of his tooth died and turned considerably darker. It seemed to bother everyone else more than it bothered him, so Johnny never did anything about it. One Father's Day the kids gave him a bag of goodies, which included an enormous bar of Toblerone chocolate. Perth's summer heat always presents a problem when it comes to storing chocolate, so Johnny cleverly, or not, placed it in the freezer. He eagerly pulled it out ready to tuck in. He bit into the first triangular division of the bar, and when he took it out, there neatly pegged into the chocolate, was the bottom piece of his tooth. It had broken off. True to form and being his usual stubborn self, he reckoned it wasn't worth the money to get it fixed. Felicity, the youngest at the time announced, 'The *tooth fairy* probably wouldn't visit to take that ugly piece.'

Apart from being a little jagged there was no real issue, according to Johnny. Every friend who saw him would ask, 'When are you going to fix your tooth?' His answer was always the same, 'I want to blend in with the tradies.' Or if a female inquisitor: 'You don't have to kiss me.'

Eventually, I think I pestered him enough that he went to the dentist. The quote was overpriced in his opinion, so he simply asked that it be removed. Many years have passed, and with each grandchild, as they get to the stage of losing their first tooth, they all gleefully compare their smile to Papa.

Epilogue

Looking back now, it almost feels as though the chapters of our lives are like a patchwork quilt, with each square sewn from a different fabric. Some squares carry bright and joyful patterns with celebrations, festivals and births. Others are darker, stitched with grief, illness or the sheer weight of uncertainty. And yet all of them, each and every one, tightly bound together by the thread of family and a strong faith.

From Zimbabwe to Australia, with a few detours through Madeira, England, and who-knows-where, our journey has never been straightforward. We have had to improvise and adjust, and often just laugh in disbelief at whatever life has thrown our way. Along the journey, we've learned to carry the stories of those who went before us; our parents, our grandparents, cousins, and so many friends. We fold all their memories into our own.

When I sit quietly and gather the scattered moments in my mind, I see a picture develop: an almost chaotic life, lived with open arms; a home filled with noisy chatter; and the quiet, unshakable knowledge that we somehow made it through together, with God on our side.

So here we are, the two of us, Johnny and Elise, with our brood of eight, and a growing number of grandchildren. We have lived and we have learned so much on this journey, now nearing four decades of our marriage. There have been dizzying highs and some valleys so low we weren't sure we'd find the way out. But hand-in-hand, with a stubborn mix of deep faith, humour and copious cups of tea, we kept moving forward.

Now that most of the kids are grown and have settled into their own lives, the grandchildren are becoming a more prominent part of the story, filling the house with new laughter and new stories.

We look back with gratitude and forward with wonder, perched between the chapters already written and those still to come.

If I have learned anything, it is this:

Life is not about the neatness of the journey but about the wonderful people we meet and travel with along the way.

What an incredible gift it has been to walk this long, winding and sometimes crazy road together with Johnny, with all its missteps, miracles, calamities and celebrations that have made us one big, messy, glorious family.

The End

EPILOGUE

J + E = 8
The Sum of Us

www.ingramcontent.com/pod-product-compliance
Lightning Source LLC
Chambersburg PA
CBHW071236070526
44583CB00017B/2214